My
Occupy

An Account
of One Person's Adventures in
the Occupy Movement

Christopher Mandel

Published by OccuBooks.org,
an imprint of Acid Kitty Productions LLC
Denver, CO

ISBN-10: 0615797792
ISBN-13: 978-0615797793

DEDICATION

For Erin, and everyone else who puts up with my craziness.

CONTENTS

INTRODUCTION

This story begins on September 1, 2011. After a year living on a farm in Oregon while finishing a Master's of Theological Studies, and then a year in Beijing teaching English, I arrived back in Denver where I had previously lived for nine years. I had no idea where my life was going. I came back to reunite with my wife, Erin, and had nothing else in mind. I quickly got a part-time job as a youth minister in a progressive Catholic Church (a very rare thing) and was looking for something to fill my time while Erin and I figured out what our next steps would be. I was out of school, back from traveling, back to married life, and after 22 years of devotion to music, had not touched my trumpet or other instruments for nine months.

Sometime in late September, Erin off-handedly mentioned some big protest which had begun in New York and was beginning to spread across the country and the world. I was immediately excited. Finally, it was happening! At last people were taking the problems of the world seriously!

I grew up in the liberal state of Oregon and then lived near Boulder, CO for several years. My whole life I've heard the proud stories of baby-boomers: "our generation fought back," "our generation changed the world," "our generation organized," "our generation was important." While I listened with respect, I found myself jealous. Why couldn't I be part of a revolution? Why couldn't my generation organize and fight back against injustice?

1

Of course, I know the reason. Two reasons really. Number one, we've been taught that organizing is a waste of time. Implicit in the stories from the 60's is a hidden message: revolution is fun, but it doesn't actually work, so don't try. And we believe it. We have no voice in the system and lack the solidarity to organize outside the system. Those few who do organize, crowd around "special interests" and never take on the big picture or the core deficiencies in our economic and political systems.

Secondly, we are comfortable. Even the poor are comfortable in America. If you are strapped for cash in America you have no voice, no healthcare, and tons of debt; but you also have a TV, a Nintendo, a computer, and as much cheap beer and fast food as you need. The oceans are dying, the national debt is growing, and your personal future is filled with troubling realities, but right now, life is pretty good. Comfortable slaves don't revolt; that's the genius of American corporate domination.

Nevertheless, starting on September 17, 2011, thousands of people across the country and the globe started seeing through this fog and rising up in an attempt to make this world a better place. This is the story of my involvement with that effort.

The first section of this book was written after the fact; while the bulk of the text comes from a journal of my day-to-day experiences. You'll notice there aren't entries for every single day but I have worked hard to write at least once or twice a week for the duration of the process.

"Why not a blog?" you may ask. "Isn't a traditional book a bit old fashioned?" Well first of all, unless you're so popular that advertisements really compound, you don't get paid for writing a blog, and while I try to be a good person doing good work, getting some compensation at the end of the day would be nice. There are many Occupiers out there writing blogs. Many publish their work with such a fast turnaround that they have to be very careful about the content they put out. If they tell the world about controversial or illegal activity within the movement, it could potentially have devastating results for themselves and their friends. For this reason, most smart bloggers self-censor a great deal and the results can sometimes read like marketing material or political propaganda.

I'm not interested in hurting my friends or the movement, but I'm also not a propagandist. My goal is to provide an honest, personal account of one person's experience in this movement, so other activists have something to compare their experiences to, and those outside the movement can peer into the Occupy world through the eyes of a participant. My goal with this project is to be fair, honest, and blatantly subjective.

I do not pretend to have the full story around everything I've been involved in. Sometimes I will recount an event and later find out that some parts of my account were wrong or incomplete. When this happens, I resist going back and editing the original entry. This means that the content should always be taken with a grain of salt. I am not a journalist. I don't shoot for objectivity; I shoot for honest story-telling.

After Erin told me about Occupy Wall Street, I researched it myself. I began getting up early every morning and taking a walk while listening to the latest Occupy news on "Democracy Now." Eventually, I looked at the Occupy Denver website. The site said they held open meetings, called general assemblies, twice a day, six days a week.

I tend to be pretty shy about getting involved in things and meeting strangers. The protest was in downtown Denver, in front of the state Capitol, so I'd drive by and watch as the number of tents in Civic Center Park rose from about five to perhaps 30. I felt guilty for not being involved. In my life I've done very little activism. I've always been opinionated and fairly well-informed. But when it comes to activism…basically it was something I always wanted to do but didn't have the motivation, courage or outlet for.

I've tried. I went to a meeting once for marijuana legalization. They were mobilizing canvassers to get a ballot measure on the Colorado ballot. I was thrilled! I took the paperwork and vowed to fill it with signatures. Two weeks later, I finally went down to the Pearl Street mall in Boulder to collect signatures but couldn't do it. I had the stuff in my backpack but didn't take it out. After an hour of trying to find the inner resources, I just headed back home.

Other than a couple anti-Desert Storm marches when I was in middle school, a marijuana decriminalization march during the 2008 Democratic Nation convention, and a disastrous two-day stint as a environmental canvasser, that was my activism until late 2011.

I went down to Civic Center Park for the first time in early October on a sunny afternoon. I stood, then sat, then meditated under the trees, from some distance, across the street from the general assembly. I didn't see any meeting really happening and I was really shy about strolling over and asking about it. There were people with signs and lots of tents. There were also a couple of tables. Frankly it looked chaotic and kind-of trashy. I just sat there for 45 minutes wishing I had the guts to move forward. Just as I had up in Boulder a few years before, I headed home.

For the next week I beat myself up. The revolution was starting and I was electing to sit it out. This would not do. "I have two choices," I told myself, "tell stories someday about how those people tried to save the world, or tell stories someday about how *we* did save the world." So the next week, despite my social neurosis, I went back to the park and walked up the sidewalk to join the crowd gathered on the steps in the little park between the state Capitol and the city building.

There were perhaps 50 people gathered in a circle. It was pre-dominately young, white, extremely alternative types, but there were others as well, including some older folks, and a few blacks and Hispanics. The group was about two-thirds male.

I also noticed a visibly drunk guy in his 40's swaying on the other side of the circle. At the time a middle-aged Native American was giving a speech about Occupy Denver proclaiming its solidarity with American Indian Movement, the Native American political organization. After he was done, people raised their hands to take turns talking about the issue[1]. My opinion at the time was that this basically consisted of a bunch young white hipsters competing over who had the most "white guilt."

It was during this time that the drunk guy gave up on standing. He passed out and hit the pavement in the middle of the circle. Someone wearing an orange medic vest appeared out of nowhere to pick him up and take him from the circle. This didn't faze the group too much; apparently they were used to such events. They quickly moved on to a vote on the statement of solidarity.

"Well, this is strange," I thought. "You guys don't even know me but you'll let me vote?" I felt uncomfortable with it, but thought,

---

[1] One of the basic procedures of general assemblies is the practice of "taking stack" wherein those who wish to speak on a particular subject raise their hands and receive a number, which designates when they may voice their thoughts. It is similar to getting a number at the DMV or Taco Bell.

"well, why not?" I voted yes, as did everyone else and the proposal unanimously passed.

My next event was a Saturday march. Every Saturday Occupy Denver held a big march starting in the park and then walking around the downtown area. I went alone as Erin's not really into this stuff and I didn't have many friends in town. I just quietly walked around with the group of several hundred passionate protesters, apprehensive about even being seen with this crowd. Other people had signs about corporations and politicians. They screamed and chanted, "Who's streets? Our streets!" and other such things, while I just hung-out and tried to avoid looking stupid.

One thing I noticed at this point was a lack of music at the march. I've been a trumpet player since I was 12 and studied music in college (I majored in music for four years, than changed to liberal studies for a fifth, in a desperate attempt to graduate). I was then a struggling wannabe pro for nine years in Colorado before giving up on it while I was in China. I saw this lack of music as a possible niche for myself. I could start a marching band for the protests, add to the movement, and reawaken my musical life. I started practicing my various instruments a couple times a week and started searching for players. At first I thought I'd quickly find interested musicians on Craigslist but my first attempt got banned within hours. I was told by a friend who frequently networks on Craigslist that this reception was what I could expect. People flag stuff they don't like and posts automatically get kicked off after a certain number of flags.

Still, I posted again. While my post didn't get flagged, it received very little attention. I only got a couple responses. I think the main problem was that marching band people don't use Craigslist much for music networking. It's mostly for people in more popular forms of music.

Between mid-October to mid-November, I also put up about 75 of flyers around college campuses and the downtown area, but never got more than six or seven people interested. They all lived in different areas of town, from the north in Boulder to south Denver, down by University of Denver. We never rehearsed. By the time I had enough people to start the next phase, there was snow on the ground. And I didn't have a tuba player. How are you going to have a marching band without a tuba? It sucks; that would have been fun, but as I write this in early February

2012, I still haven't put together that band nor have I resurrected my musical life.

At my first general assembly I managed to vote. I think it was at...oh, wait...first I need to mention the first raid. A few days after my first GA, the tent city[2] protest was broken up by the authorities. I wasn't there, but everyone in town and even the nation heard about it. It was one of the first big police actions to force out an occupation.

On the southern end of the downtown area of Denver is Colfax, a long east/west, four-lane street notorious for prostitution and drugs. On the southern side of this street are the city building, the state Capitol, the jail, and the US mint. Between the state Capitol and the city building, there are two parks, side by side, divided by Broadway. On the east side is a state park, which held the Occupation in the first month of the protest. To the west, is Civic Center Park, which is city property.

The police action was huge. There were scores of cops, hundreds maybe; I don't know. Many had full riot garb on. They pushed the protesters out of the state park, took all the tents and tables, and arrested 20 or so people.

I watched it on my computer. It was crazy! Batons. Tear gas. Pepper bullets[3]. I saw a video featuring a protester throwing food at a cop who was just standing there looking intimidating. "Peaceful protest?" I thought; throwing food counts as violence in my book.

The next general assembly that I went to was held in Civic Center Park. Across the way, the state park was devoid of people except for several cop cars. Through the next several weeks, the park on the state-owned side of Broadway had at least three police cars in it at all times.

The look of the new occupation was totally different. There were still lots of people and a few tables. The Thunderdome[4] was still present, and

---

[2] The ongoing protest in the park with tents and sleeping bags goes by several names. It can be referred to as "the physical occupation," "the 24/7 occupation," and in later months it went by "the Row."

[3] Pepper bullets are a preferred form of nonlethal deterrence for today's police forces. They are similar to paintballs but instead of containing paint, they contain liquid pepper spray and from what I can tell, are fired by conventional paint ball guns.

[4] The Thunderdome was the kitchen area that freely fed anyone who asked, day or night. It wasn't exactly sanitary but they were certainly nice. They fed dozens of people, mostly homeless folks, every day. It began simply as an eating area for Occupiers, but eventually evolved into a separate organization.

the park was filled with people, but it held no tents or structures. All large items were on the sidewalk. Every day at 11:00 pm, the park closed and a team of police swept everyone out, arresting anyone who didn't comply. Therefore, the protesters kept their things on the sidewalk, where they would sleep at night.

There were no tents to be found. While the city had little recourse for stopping people from sleeping on the sidewalk, they could ban tents. Tents, they claimed, are buildings and therefore subject to zoning and building codes. The protest crossed the street to the city park and abandoned the state side. Hence, the west side of Broadway was lined with tarps and sleeping bags. And no tents.

I think it was at my second or third general assembly that I had a thought, "You know, these guys don't need a band. They need some real help organizing." My original thought was that the band would be my voice in the movement but it was obvious that there were more important roles. The park was full of well-meaning people but there was little form to it all. No way to deal with donations. No way to plan long-term goals. No system for internal communication. No way to collectively find a path and stick to it. So I decided to step in deeper than I originally envisioned.

It was also my second or third GA where I made my first-ever announcement. I messed up and spoke during the wrong part of the meeting but no one said anything.[5] I announced that I was starting the band and that I could use some help. I was really hoping to get some support from Occupy Denver and to find some individuals who would help, but it didn't happen. In fact it was like no one noticed I spoke. I felt completely ignored.

A professional looking woman in her 30's also made an announcement. She was starting a committee to find a headquarters where we could meet, store things, and escape to if we got raided again. After the meeting I intro-duced myself and joined her group. She explained that, like me, she knew no one and had only come to a couple general assemblies before that. She

---

[5] Contrary to popular belief, Occupy General Assemblies are highly organized. The details of the structure vary from Occupation to Occupation but are generally fairly similar. There will be announcements, often split into subtypes such as committee announcements and outside group announcements; agenda items, which are official proposals for the group to debate and vote on; and sometimes discussion topics.

felt that since the group obviously needed a physical home, she decided to start the committee; this sounded good to me so I gave her my email. This was my first inclusion on to an OD committee.

It was at this time that I started to understand Occupy better. There is no hierarchy. There are no gate-keepers. If you want to do something, you just do it. The ladder between being a no-name, no power, no-nothing, to being important, respected, and influential isn't a ladder at all. It's just an adjustment in your own thinking. If you want to change the world through the Occupy movement, you can. There's no establishment shutting you out.

In most walks of life there is an explicit or implicit chain of events which must occur for you to have any influence. You need the right educ-ation. You need experience in the field. You need a license, certificate, or permit. Often you need a bunch of cash, the right friends, or even a particular nationality, race, or gender. But in Occupy, this isn't the case. In Occupy, the only things limiting you are your own motivation and talent. When this dawned on me, I realized that this was my chance. Through Occupy, I finally had the opportunity to do something with this little life of mine.

I didn't start out too well though. My first projects were the band and the Headquarters Committee. The band never got off the ground and I was never active in HQ. I tried to be helpful in email chains but I never actually did anything. This fellow Jesse, who was the first person I met through the movement, found a house in north Denver but it needed a ton of work done to it. I tried to find time to help; I didn't want to dodge the work, but I never made it up there.

By mid-November I was going to several general assemblies a week but still spoke little and didn't know many people. One night, the group decided to form a finance Committee for managing the ample donations we were receiving at the time. This group was unique among the committees. Its members would be elected. The idea was to nominate people on Wed-nesday and then elect five people the following Friday.

I had no real interest in the committee and no qualifications, but the facilitator[6] of the GA was begging people to become nominees, so I jumped

---

[6] General Assemblies have several designated roles which are filled on the spot by volunteers. These include the Facilitator, who guides the flow of the meeting; the Stack-

in. There were a total of 19 nominees, so I figured there was no chance I'd get picked. After all, no one knew me and I wasn't qualified.

Well…I showed up on Friday and the field had narrowed to five nominees. Since we needed five, the facilitator simply asked the circle if anyone had a problem with any of the nominees. No one complained so all five of us got on. This was my second committee.

Finance held a meeting soon after. Of the five of us, three had professional experience and one was a professor who had written books about alternative economics. There was the tall, lanky Tad. He was probably in his early 30's and had some business-y job. He seemed to know what he was doing and he made it to almost all of the 7:00 pm GAs. Josh was a young good-looking hippy from Boulder who also had some finance knowledge. Wiley was a Muslim woman in her late 30's, or early 40's who wore a traditional headscarf over her bright green hair, and was a professor. Finally, there was Dwayne, who had no finance background. He was a big black guy, about 50 years old, who often gave passionate, articulate speeches in GA. He lived here on the street and rarely left the occupation. Due to his constant presence, and the fact that he came off as the kind of dude you don't mess around with, he was very useful to the committee. He had an important role in dealing with the cash donations we got on the street from passing cars. At the time, we were getting about $100 a day this way, so watching that dough was a big responsibility. My job was to stay out of the way and try not to be an asshole.

At this point, I'd been involved for three or four weeks. I kept thinking that the movement lacked a long-term plan. At every GA there were basically three focuses:

1. Organizing events and committees (new committees were springing up every week).
2. Dealing with the basic day-to-day survival of the people living on the street and the movement itself.
3. Some weirdo conspiracy guy going off about radiation in the water or Obama's ties to Russian/alien hybrids.

Taker, who organizes the order in which people may speak and tallies votes; the Note-Taker, who takes notes and publishes them later; and we occasionally use a Vibes Watcher, who jumps in when the meeting gets contentious or off track.

There was no talk about big-picture stuff. Even real politics was a secondary topic of speech. We all just took it for granted that we were there for the same reasons.

I was beginning to dream about a group that would be essentially a think-tank. It would just talk and research heavy big-picture stuff; and when appropriate, it would create proposals based on that work which could lend some long-term planning to the movement. One night at GA, some guy proposed a group to write an "Occupy Constitution." This project seemed similar to mine so I got on stack and told the 30 or so people at GA about my idea for a "big-picture" group. Then Terese, a petite girl in her mid 20's, piped up and said she was planning on starting a group to work on a "Declaration of Purpose."

The GA was generally confused by three similar but different proposals coming up at the same time. It quickly moved on to other matters and left the three of us to work out integrating our ideas. Terese was, in my view, one of the leading organizers of Occupy Denver. She was at nearly every GA, spoke often, and facilitated several General Assemblies a week. She was, I felt, an OD insider.

When the three of us met after the GA ended, something strange happened. Terese directed all of her attention to me and ignored the other fellow, who was desperately trying to participate in the conversation, but struggling to do so. I was quite aware of this strange dynamic in the conversation and attempted to include the guy, but for Terese he was invisible.

Let me explain. I'm used to being ignored. I'm used to being the invisible guy left wondering whether I'm really physically incarnated or a ghostly apparition. I'm not used to being pulled aside as someone worth talking to. While I felt for Mr. Invisible, I was also flattered and excited by the attention given by Terese. This meant I was breaking through! Someone who mattered noticed me! Terese went on to become a good friend. Mr. Invisible...I never saw again.

This little meeting led to an email chain and culminated two weeks later when Terese and I proposed the formation of a drafting group for an Occupy Denver Declaration of Purpose. We began with a motivational speech by me and then she introduced the details of the group. While I had gotten on stack and cautiously given my opinion a few times at GA, this was my first prepared speech. Actually it was pretty much the first public speech I'd ever given.

The proposal easily passed and I found myself a member of my third official Occupy Denver group. And unlike HQ and Finance, I left the gate as one of the organizers of the project. This was about a month after my first GA.

One consistent theme in Occupy Denver has always been the delicate relationship between the GA and its committees, and the Row. By mid-November there was a constant undercurrent of tension between the two.

In the beginning, the General Assembly was a way for physical Occupiers to communicate. Since Occupy is a non-hierarchical people's movement, the meetings were open to the general public. Soon people like me started showing up; that is people who wanted to be involved but were not willing to sleep on the sidewalk every night. By mid-November these "part-timers" substantially outnumbered the "full-timers." This led to resentment on the part of the full-timers who felt that they were the "real Occupiers" and that these wimpy, wannabe activists were co-opting the movement.

During November it was quite common for someone aligned with the 24/7 Occupiers to barge into the middle of GA and start screaming that the GA was a meaningless "circle-jerk" and was doing nothing to help the real Occupation.

It should be stated that there was some truth to this. Almost all of our energy at that time was put into building bureaucracy. New committees were constantly popping up. Sometimes they would quickly die an unnoticed death, while others would become the foundation of the organization. And sometimes, as was the case with the Security Committee, everyone assumed there was a committee because the need was so great, but in fact there wasn't one.

To alleviate the growing communication problem between committees, an Administrative Committee was started. It was their job to build structures connecting the various projects going on. But this proved far more challenging than anyone anticipated. Occupiers are cats! Not just cats…they are pissed-off, anarchist, anti-authoritarian cats who want to bring down the system. On one hand, everyone desperately wanted more organization (someone going off in GA about how we needed more organization happened several times a week.) But no one wanted hierarchy of any kind, which meant these structures could not come down from a governing body. They had to come organically from the people and be passed by GA, that way GA (which represents the 99%) always had ultimate control. Due to this dynamic, the bureaucracy building process took endless hours of GA time and the physical Occupation often became an afterthought.

I felt guilty about being an "armchair activist" or "circle-jerk GA snob." And I felt troubled by the disconnect between the 24/7 Occupation and the GA. It seemed to reflect the kind of class boundary we all wanted to end. We in the GA tried to ignore it but the reality was obvious: probably 75% of the 24/7's were people who would be homeless regardless of the protest while 75% of typical GA participants had college degrees and jobs.

Sadly, as you might expect, the GA crowd always avoided the topic and when forced into addressing it, would tend to diminish the topic, creating rhetoric of solidarity with the homeless and the 24/7 Occupiers. The 24/7's, on the other hand, either screamed that they wanted to be included and that the GA needed to give them more support or they totally dismissed the GA as simply another manifestation of elitist domination. At this point, a few ambassadors became increasingly important. Most important was Ben, a young man of mixed black/white racial background. He was articulate and passionate about the needs of the homeless. Educated and generally employed, he lived on the street purely as a political statement and, thankfully, despite his frustration with GA, he participated anyway.

It was at this time that I decided to start staying the night on the street once a week. I was a bit scared of doing this but one night I packed up my sleeping bag and some clothes and stuffed them in my hiking backpack along with a flashlight, my Nintendo DS, and a traveler's mug full of warm coffee and rum.

Once I arrived at the Occupation around 11:00 pm, I immediately became aware that there was simply no way I was going to sleep there.

There was just no way. But I'm a night owl and I didn't mind the idea of staying up all night with a protest sign in my hand.

It's funny, hanging out with the crazy people and drunks didn't bring up any fear in me. Having a background in the New Age movement, I've been around my fair share of crazies. As for the drunks and stoners…well, my general strategy was to join them.

My resistance was toward holding a sign. I don't know why. I can only say that it keyed into my general shyness and fear of being noticed. In four weeks of activism, I'd managed to avoid holding a sign but, once again, I managed to break through my fears. I found an adequately attractive sign lying on the ground and spent about half the night sitting in my chair holding the sign while playing video games on my DS or phone and waving to honking cars.

The other half of the time is when I got to know the other side of Occupy Denver. There were all these people there I didn't know but who knew one another and seemed to identify themselves as Occupiers. They tended to gather around the Thunderdome and a portable barbeque which was used for a little bonfire. The flame was generally kept low because whenever it grew higher than a foot, the police, who had numerous cars all the way around the encampment, would come tell us to keep it down.

I stayed the night three times in late November and early December. I can't quite remember what happened when, so I'll just give a run-down of some of the people I met and adventures I had. Here are a few of our characters:

Gangsta Billy. Billy was a huge, muscular black man. He was a constant presence at the Occupation and his voice could be heard seemingly at all times. He loved loudly singing popular tunes or just making up new ones with his deep, rusty voice. At some point he was given a djembe hand drum and from then on he was never seen without it. Billy had the unique ability to completely ignore the cold. Even in snow, he'd often run around without his shirt singing, playing his drum, and insisting that all that witness his glory, "respect his gangsta."

Once I was in a bar with Ben when he suggested that GA should officially pass a resolution that OD respects Billy's gangsta. I said that I was cool with this proposal but that I felt my "hipster douche bag" was equally impressive and should also be officially recognized.

<u>Crazy Jesus Lady</u>. Nicole was a young homeless woman. While on her meds she was compassionate, loving, and politically articulate. When she was off her meds, she ran around in the middle of traffic and swung her Bible and her Christian faith like she was fighting an army of demons. Despite her incredibly annoying preaching and habit of grabbing the attention of the police, she was loved by everyone in the Occupation and tended to symbolize the plight of the homeless.

Sadly, one evening we got the news that Nicole had passed away due to exposure on a cold, snowy night. Many people were distraught while others just asked, "Who's Nicole?" This was rather controversial because it put a bright spotlight on the tensions between the Row and the GA.

After a couple of days, a vigil was organized and about 20 Occupiers, mostly members of the Row but also a few organizers, walked down the 16th Street Mall with candles lit to pay tribute to Nicole and the struggles of the homeless in general. About a week latter Nicole showed up asking what all the fuss was about.

<u>Hare Krishna Guy</u>. Hare Krishna Guy was tall, black, quite young, and beautiful. This flamboyantly gay man had a gorgeous voice that rang out praise to Lord Krishna night and day. He was also, like Billy and Nicole, totally crazy.

Between the rough dirges of Gangsta Billy and the melodious devotion of Hare Krishna Guy, the occupation was always full in song, often times, even late at night.

Most of the others in this scene were a bit less dramatic. Many were older people, mostly men, who you knew had been on the street for a while. There were also younger street people who were generally in better shape.

I was once standing around the fire when a middle-aged Native American man politely walked up to the fire and asked if anyone had a phone. I said I did and offered it to him. He was holding his side and explained that he was in pain and needed an ambulance.

I want to say that I am terrible in these situations. Where the hell was Ben!? He's the courageous hero who stays level-headed, has seen these situations countless times before, and knows what to do and when to do it!

The guy started to get worse and laid down in the middle of the sidewalk groaning, still holding my phone. He called 911 but was unable to talk. I took the phone and attempted to explain the situation. I explained that the dude was in pain and needed help. The lady asked where I was and I said the Occupy protest. She asked for an address or street intersection. I was like "I'm at the fucking Occupy protest, don't you read the newspaper!?" Ok, I didn't actually say that. I managed to say we were on Broadway and Colfax.

I swear I heard the siren 30 seconds later. Within five minutes the dude was being hauled into the back of an ambulance. A couple days later I asked a few people what had happened to him, but no one knew. I never heard how he did.

The Thunderdome got all of its supplies via donation. Random people who were sympathetic with the movement would drive by, stop, and hand us supplies from their trunk or backseat. The food area was generally well-stocked but occasionally ran out of something crucial. I was there once at about 1:00 am when the Thunderdome ran out of water.

This middle-aged, very sweet homeless man explained that he knew where a water tap was and that he wanted to lead a group to it. So four of us picked up as many big water bottles as possible and followed him. As we went, it became clear that one of my companions, a fellow in his 20s with had a handlebar mustache and a brown 70's suit, was not completely stable. He kept running off, stopping, or getting really noisy. Whenever this happened the older guy would redirect him toward the water or remind him that it was nighttime and he should be quiet. It was clear to me that this fellow took care of mentally unstable people all the time. He seemed to take the situation for granted and see himself as their caretaker.

We made it back with the water without a problem, despite being followed by a cop car the whole way and the crazy antics of 70's Suit Guy. I talked to the older gentleman quite a bit that night. He explained to me that he knew God was real and that if he truly wanted something, God would always give it to him. His life, he explained was quite happy and he had all he needed.

A common occurrence, while I sat in my folding camping chair holding a beaten up protest sign and raising my fist in the air every time a car beeped as it flew by, was for people to pass by and talk to me about politics and the movement. Generally on these nights I appeared to the average, middleclass Denverite to be the safest and sanest person in the street (little did they know), so it was always me they'd approach.

Most often people were cool. The most common conversation would involve people bitching about the current state of the country and thanking me and the movement for doing what we were doing. It was also quite common for people to simply ask questions, "Why don't you guys use tents?" "Why are you really here?" "What are you hoping Occupy leads to?" "Are all these homeless people really protesters?"

But sometime people weren't so cool. One time a group of three 30- and 40-something men came up to me and started asking me about the occupation. They were out on the town after a Broncos game and in a cheerful, beer-lubricated mood. They said they were into the politics of what we were doing but thought we didn't know what we were doing and ultimately wouldn't accomplish anything. One in particular swung his arm in a gesture toward the people sleeping on the street, and said "Bend, Oregon has an occupation twice this size. Why are you so small?" I said, "Well, I'm happy for Bend. But I'll bet they've never been attacked by an army of riot police."

This took the men aback for a moment, but they soon went into, "You guys should be more organized." "You guys should get a leader." "You guys should clean up the park." "You guys should focus on one issue." I was pissed off but remained polite. My function on the street was as a representative of the movement and yelling at some drunk assholes wasn't going to help the cause, so I just said we were working on that stuff.

Here are the top five ways to piss off an Occupier:

5) Fire pepper bullets or tear gas at them.
4) Pass a law restricting free speech on the internet or condoning warrantless surveillance.
3) Lobby congress to give the corporate interests you work for unfair advantages.
2) Be a congressman who takes money from the afore-mentioned lobbyist.
1) Start a sentence with "You guys should….."

To all those who know what we should be doing, all I can say is, "Good point; help us do it."

One interesting effect this movement has had is its impact on the implications and possible uses of the word "occupy." This word has come in our society to have automatic political implications and will never be a nice, neutral word ever again.

I was sitting down on a piece of cardboard on Broadway and Colfax when the full scope of semantic possibilities for this word was demonstrated for me. I was hanging out with some street kids who were playing with their puppy and making up little songs with a beaten-up guitar.

At one point, one pulled out a bag of chips and started munching away. One of his companions asked, "What's that you're occupying there?" And he replied, "I'm occupying some nacho cheese Doritos! You need some?" Later, as was common, a car drove by and someone yelled from the window, "Get a job!" The same young man threw back, "Occupy your mom!"

DECEMBER

I had some of the most disturbing, exciting, inspiring, and educational experiences of my life, all crammed within the period between late September and late November 2011. This being the case, I came to the conclusion that I should record as much of what I was seeing as possible. Hence, I'm now shifting from the narrative, told several months later (I wrote most of the last section in early February 2012), to journaling.

12/4/11

Today I had my third youth group meeting scheduled but only two kids showed up, so we canceled it. The problem...I had about 20 cookies I did NOT want at my house, so off I went to the Sunday general assembly. It was snowing hard, and everyone was bundled up, jumping around to fend off the cold.

The main agenda item was how to deal with the event Cory and Neal had proposed several days before regarding shutting down a Wal-Mart distribution plant in Loveland, which is about 60 miles away. It turned out that I wasn't alone in my frustration over their strategy for influencing Occupy Denver. On the contrary, about half the people there were pissed off about the whole thing and didn't really want to do it, but...what do you do? GA approved it, so it goes forward.

Worse yet, there are two other events being held at the same time. One is this cool "Tea Bag the Governor's office" thing. People are just going to stroll up to the Capitol building and throw tea at it! Sounds like silly fun! The other event is closing a distribution plant in Commerce City, which is far closer to the occupation than the Loveland event. Several people, including myself, suggested that we simply forget the Loveland event and concentrate in Commerce City, but it didn't happen.

Did I mention that all of this was happening with a Crazy Jesus Lady repeatedly throwing herself into the middle of the ring of people? She was holding a big sign she'd made and would occasionally scream about her freedom of religion. Every time she did this, we'd just ignore her for a while and then someone would gather her up, coax her back to the edge, only to see her jump back into the middle a few moments later. There was also this young homeless guy who interrupted the meeting with, "Attention, attention! Whoever stole my sleeping bag needs to give it back. It's all I have. That's not cool." He did this two or three times. I didn't know what to think, sucks for him, but I didn't do it.

12/6/11

I went to a meeting for Occupy DU (University of Denver) tonight. Roshan put it together. That guy is on about three committees with Occupy Denver, goes to almost every GA and facilitates many of them, and now is building a separate group at the University of Denver. He's obviously very tired and frustrated. He's come to the conclusion that he needs to carry the movement on his back, but the consequences are that he's irritable and exhausted. That dude seriously needs a day off.

The meeting had a totally different vibe than what I'm used to seeing. It was all young, snotty students. Some were already gung-ho about the movement but some were there to learn more and were actually a bit skeptical.

Several asked what the movement was about; what are its goals or demands. We named a few of the usual answers. We (Roshan and I) each expressed that Occupy is not a special interest group; it is a broad reform movement. Roshan said that there is a push to pigeon-hole the group into a small set of specific interests and that this was ultimately a method by the media and the government to placate us. First they give us a nice, small, specific interest, thereby pushing out those who don't care about that particular issue from the conversation. Then they have some kind of public debate where the two political sides try to pin all the problems onto the other and take credit for any attempts to address the problem. Finally they pass some watered-down, essentially symbolic bill that doesn't fix the problems but may trick the masses into believing things will get better. We've seen this pattern with healthcare, budget responsibility, and climate change, to name just a few examples.

I, at one point, gave my speech about how Occupy is an "imperfect revolution." I said something like, "There are problems. There are conflicts. People don't always agree and sometimes things move too slowly or GA gets frustrating. But this is THE revolution. It's an imperfect revolution, but it's the only game in town. It's really a yes or no question: are you in or out? There isn't another revolution out there to join."

This blond girl from the School of International Studies said that she, for one, didn't like the idea of a revolution and that she felt we were being inconsistent on whether we wanted revolution or reform. Furthermore, she said that in her country (America), "we have a revolution every four years where the people have the opportunity to replace the current leaders."

It was interesting to hear the voices of those who don't agree with us. I still believe what I believe, but it's nice to step back and hear other points of view.

12/7/11

I am so tired. Last night was a crazy general assembly. I began it by telling GA about the $1500 donation I've been working on. The problem is that the donor, the online news source, Nation of Change, is demanding a detailed list about how the money will be spent, but OD doesn't have a mechanism for creating such a list. The GA gave me a few ideas for how to deal with the situation, and then went on to other matters. This is when things went downhill.

Becca, who was essentially pushed out of the movement about a month and a half ago, proposed that GA give committees permission to make proposals at GA meetings. She said this was coming because some of her friends had been told at committee meetings that it wasn't ok to talk about proposals. We took stack. Then every single person said basically the same thing: "Of course committees can bring proposals to GA. It happens all the time; why are we even talking about this?!"

Now Becca's not very popular. From what I understand, she had been basically voted off the island at one point and now she wasn't helping her reputation. Al said something like, "don't take this the wrong way. But right now, I basically want to punch you in the face for making us talk about this."

At this time Roshan, who was facilitating, started screaming at Al for making personal attacks at GA. We went through the stack, with everyone saying the same stuff, and Becca defending herself. Someone called to go to vote, I seconded, but others didn't want to vote on what was seen as a non-issue. More people wanted to talk but the stack keeper and facilitator didn't want to go on.

Liberty, the stack keeper, went around the circle again to take stack but was begging people not to raise their hands. Some stranger started criticizing the GA for not being able to work together, which just got people more pissed off. People everywhere were yelling or starting side conversations and Roshan was just trying to get things back in control. This is when I jumped stack[7] and yelled, "This sucks, let's move on!," people cheered and we simply stopped the conversation and moved on to the next item.

This didn't help though. The next item was organizing for the December 12th Wal-Mart event that no one actually wants to do. Cory and Neal were getting pissed that the PR committee wasn't promoting the event, so they brought the event organization to GA. I don't know how it happened but this topic led to conflict as well.

At this point, I left the circle to talk about finance stuff with Tad and Adrianne. Tad has continued to keep me and Josh out of the loop on finance matters which irritates Josh to no end. Now Adrianne has one of only two cards for the bank account while I and Josh do not. Adrianne having access is perfectly acceptable. She is a member of the Administration Committee and a very talented and cool person. But I'm pretty sure she and Tad are dating, and it makes me nervous that the only people with access to the bank account are a couple.

---

[7] "Jumping stack" is talking out of turn.

Anyway, Tad and Josh can't make it to the 12/12 protest. Wiley is taking a break. Dwayne isn't going either. This means it's my job to go up to the protest in Loveland, avoid getting arrested, and bail people out of jail after the event. If this thing turns into a full-on blockade, we could really be looking at arrests. I won't lie; I'm not comfortable with this responsibility.

As we were having this meeting, GA started getting loud again. I turned my head to see Roshan yelling to Cory that he needed to stop with the personal attacks. Cory's arm was out in front of him with his middle finger extended upward, while he was saying, "This is not a personal attack." I love it when GA is like this!

Later that night we went out for beer. Ben spent the first hour bitching about Cory and the next half hour bitching about Shelby the Dog[8]. He also talked about the latest of a series of meetings he is having with the mayor. Unbeknownst to most of Occupy Denver, Ben is actually getting things done. It was during this post GA party that I saw the latest issue of WestWord, the local independent newspaper. On the cover was Cory dressed as Don Quixote holding a three-foot bong.

12/9/11

Yesterday The Declaration of Purpose drafting group held a meeting in the library just south of Civic Center Park. There were about ten people there, all of whom were enthusiastic about constructing a statement about the intent of Occupy Denver. In the last two months several Occupy groups have issued general statements about what Occupy is all about but none have built any nationwide traction.

Writing a nice statement about why Occupy Denver exists would not be hard. We could simply pick a writer, give them some ideas, and let him or her construct the thing. The problem is that a document created this way wouldn't reflect the group mentality of the movement and would undoubtedly skew toward the beliefs of the author. We want to do something more substantial than that; we want something truly reflecting the ideas of the collective.

---

[8] Shelby is a border collie who is at the occupation on a regular basis. As a statement about corporate personhood and as a response to criticism that Occupy needs leadership, OD recently elected her as the official leader of Occupy Denver. The move was controversial but yielded a fair bit of press coverage.

As a first step we decided to conduct a survey, so we can include the ideas of as many Occupiers as possible. Upon this decision we spent the next two hours drafting the leading question for the survey. How did we spend two hours working on one question? As a group we negotiated every word of the short statement! This sentence is too long. No it's too short. That word seems pretentious. Let's use a semi-colon instead of a period. It was a strange process but did the job; we ended up with a nice lead question:

> The 99% of Denver stand for and against many differrent things. We face a variety of problems, and we sometimes differ on causes and solutions. But the more we work together, the more effective we can be. Too easily, our common call can be lost among the many voices that we represent. That is why Occupy Denver is seeking input on a Statement of Purpose. We hope that it will serve as a starting point for a much needed conversation on what this movement is about. It will not be the sole message of Occupy Denver, but it will help others understand us, help us understand ourselves, and ensure that we stay grounded in what we all have in common.
>
> As part of this process, we want input from people like you so that the statement accurately represents the 99%. So we ask that you share your explanation, in simple terms, of what this movement is about. In 150 words or less, either using prose form or no more than 5 bullet points, please answer the following question:
>
> **If Occupy Denver were completely successful, what would that success look like?**

Today, on the way back home from Broomfield, I was thinking about a proposal I've been concocting for a while. I felt that OD needs to start an integrated campaign for growth, at the expense of other priorities. I devised a month and a half period where all committees make growth top priority.

Despite having planed earlier on taking the day off, I decided that tonight was the night for the proposal. So I went.

Surprisingly the only push-back came from Roshan and Terese, who felt that growth was already the top priority and that the proposal didn't have any real content. To alleviate this problem, Roshan suggested an amendment that all committees be required to have a conversation about the topic and submit a statement about that conversation to the Administrative Committee, who would disseminate it. With this addition, it easily passed. Now we'll see if it does anything. I'm hoping it leads to a concentrated attack on this issue and helps things quite quickly but, as Roshan implied, it could easily just fall into the dead-meaningless proposals abyss. We'll see.

12/11/11

So I'm a little behind on this journal. I want to keep it up but some-times there's just so much going on. Right now it's all about the Wal-Mart action tomorrow. Thursday I was at an Outreach meeting. What I missed was a long emergency GA regarding a rumor about a car bombing being planned for the event. Jesus… I talked to Joe about it Saturday, who assured me that there was never such a plan.

On Wednesday, Cory, Anthony, and Tanner were brainstorming ideas for the event. Someone said, "Maybe we could blockade the road with a car." This led to Anthony unwisely saying, "I've got a car I don't need; maybe we could start it on fire. Wouldn't that be cool?" They got excited and went to Rob, who's in the Legal Committee and is a former police officer, to ask his opinion. He replied, "What the fuck are you thinking?! That could be construed as terrorist activity. You could be living the rest of your lives in a jail cell!" So then the idea died.

However, later that night it ended up on the OD Twitter feed that the three were planning on a car bomb. There were phone calls made and the announcement was taken down but not before the news was all over Twitter. From what I can gather, there are many versions of this story and even now a certain amount of uncertainty about whether they were true. I just talked to Cat, who said she would probably avoid the event just to be on the safe side. How many other people are saying the same thing I wonder?

Yesterday I was at the occupation and Neal started going off about assholes in GA and assholes in the PR Committee. After he calmed down, he explained that the website had published his personal and business information. He requested that it be taken off, which it was, but it later went back up. In connection to the car bomb rumor, his business was visited by Federal officers and this somehow led to a $200 fine.

The money isn't that big a deal, but Neal is very scared about the Feds getting into his personal and business life and feels that he has enemies within the PR Committee, which he does. A few days ago after GA, he and Cory were frustrated with the lack of support they were getting for the 12/12 protest and they made nasty remarks about the PR Committee, which left one girl in tearful hysterics. PR has been under a lot of criticism for several weeks and this, apparently, was too much. It sent her into a screaming tirade about how she'd been accused of being an undercover agent.

This week I've been exhausted with this stuff. Everyone is working too hard. There's lot of anger and mistrust within our own ranks. There is a lot of anxiety about the 12/12 protest. Did you notice that it's happening tomorrow? I feel like it's the end of Westside Story and everything come downs to "Tonight," only the song goes "Tomorrow… aaaaall day."

12/13/11

I'm tired and have been doing Occupy stuff all day. Just like yesterday. One of the day's tasks was a little art project. The Declaration of Purpose group printed out a few dozen copies of the survey, but had no place to store them safely at the snowy occupation, so it was assigned to me to build a box which could stay in the park where people could turn in completed forms. I decided to have some fun with it and turned it into a bigger project than it had to be. First I built the box itself out of cardboard and added a slit were the forms could be dropped. I then decorated it. I found a photo of the actual Declaration of Independence, printed it off and taped it to the front and sides. I then covered the rest with an old copy of Occupy the Press, the Denver-based Occupy newspaper. Finally I printed a copy of the question and a description of the project, and placed it near the slit. I'll take it down to the park next time I'm there.

I'll bet you're wondering about the Wal-Mart action. Ok, here we go: I got to the occupation around 8:30 am. There was a group of people yelling about money. They seemed to be afraid of running into Ben because he was super pissed-off. That's great…what a way to start the day. There weren't many people there and I took this to be a bad sign. I ran into Cory who embarrassingly said he wasn't going. Due to the car bomb stuff, he was afraid to show his face at the event. Ben wasn't going; Roshan, Terese, and Neal all had the same story. Of the people I tend to consider major organizers, none were going.

I drove up with two homeless Occupiers in the car: Crazy and Drew Kerry. That's Kerry with a "K." His name isn't legally changed yet, but he's working on it. Drew Kerry is a young man of 19 years who just came here from Colorado Springs. Drew Kerry loves Denver. Drew Kerry speaks in the third person. Drew Kerry thinks this is the best song in the world and Crazy and Chris should quit talking and listen to it. Drew Kerry has been arrested eight times in the last six months and Drew Kerry wants to write my phone number on his arm so I can find him after Drew Kerry gets arrested today.

Crazy is a pretty young woman who seems reasonably intelligent and well-spoken. As well as being a full-time Occupier, she is heavily involved in the Rainbow Gathering. She is the biological mother of one child and has three more she helps take care of. I really don't know what this means, since she spends so much time at the occupation and I don't see any kids around. In any case, I like her and found her kind-of exotically attractive. At one point I noticed her hands are very calloused and rough.

We got to Loveland around 10:00 am. There were about 50 protesters from Denver, Fort Collins, Greeley, and Boulder. There were also about 30 cops. Several were very friendly, average-looking police officers who talked to us and even gave out a few of those police badge stickers. About ten were riot guys with those pepper-ball guns. The final ten were on horseback.

It was very tame and there was a general vibe of disappointment at the poor showing. Crazy and Drew Kerry weren't bored though. Drew Kerry wrote "Occupy Wal-Mart" or something on his chubby belly and flashed cars that went by. Crazy wrote "Occupy my Gangster" on the back of her pants and would bend over to show the text to drivers.

At about 12:45 pm I went back to my car a half-mile away to get some food and take a nap. At 1:30 I got a call from Cat. I said, "Everything's fine; boring actually." Cat, who was back in Denver, said "Ten people just got arrested." I was thinking, "Oh shit! Busted!"

I ran down there and the excitement was all over but the chaos remained. I tried to get the names of the people arrested but half of them had street nicknames. Someone finally shows me a list. There are 12 people. Near the end of the list was Mr. Drew Kerry. Luckily, over the next hour most of these folks walked back up the street to rejoin the protest.

Apparently, law enforcement wanted to make a big show of taking away the protesters that attempted to blockade the Wal-Mart trucks from leaving and entering the distribution plant, but they didn't actually arrest them. Instead the police drove them to a parking lot about a mile away, ticketed them for impeding traffic and then let them go. Only four people were actually arrested, two of which were Occupy Denver folks who had prior warrants.

For the next two hours I was on and off the phone notifying and, at times, being notified by Liberty and Cat back in Denver about what is going on. By 3:00 pm, the protest was dissipating and Drew Kerry and I headed home listening to loud hip-hop. Technically, Drew Kerry only got ticketed for jay-walking, but Drew Kerry is proudly saying that Drew Kerry has now been arrested nine times in the past six months.

After getting back to Denver, I went to GA. I arrived a little late and found the group in a heated argument over who would facilitate the meeting. Jesus, really? After another 20 minutes of arguing, Caryn (who had gotten a ticket for obstructing a vehicle just six hours earlier) ran across the circle in an attempt to attack Becca, the would-be facilitator. People, please…

Today I spent all day dealing with the arrests, researching alternatives to PayPal (PayPal helped bring down WikiLeaks and therefore is no friend to us, in my opinion), researching printers we could buy, and responding to Occu-email. Then I went to GA. The first hour concentrated on a meeting the new Denver sheriff wants to have with us. The stack went 20 deep for some reason and after that, the meeting broke down and people just starting talking over each other. Roshan was facilitating and eventually got it under control. Totally exasperated, he pushed it to a vote and only one person voted against the proposal as it originally stood: "I propose that five or six committee members have a meeting with the new sheriff sometime in the next two days." Fucking GA. O Lord, forgive the GA, it knows not what it does. This was such a no-brainer; it shouldn't have taken more than five minutes of discussion.

I'm also still trying to spend this $1500 from Nation of Change. I can't believe it's this hard to SPEND money! Every time a good idea for how to spend it comes up, someone says, "Maybe we can get it donated." I want to scream, "It IS fucking donated! The $1500 is do-fucking-nated dough!" I should send Nation of Change an email; I've been putting it off.

Tomorrow: bondsman conversation, visit from a middle-school classroom, and possibly a meeting with the sheriff.

12/14/11

The school visit was fantastic! It made me feel better about this movement than I've felt in a couple of weeks. There were about six Occupiers there and a group of about 20 fourth- and fifth-graders from a private school. We gave a question/answer presentation and then held a general assembly with the kids. Since they are part of the 99%, we decided to make it a real GA with the power to make binding decisions.

With our help, the kids passed two proposals. One was for their class to donate scrap cardboard and art to the occupation. The other one was for us to make a video about the occupation and include some of them in it. Boy, it was fun! They figured out the process very quickly and really made it their own.

Like yesterday, I spent all day doing Occupy work on the computer. Then in the afternoon, I received a text: "Fwd: people at the Occupy Denver encampment were handed eviction notices by the public works department today saying they would be evicted tomorrow. We need all hands on deck at GA tonight to figure out how to respond. Please spread the word."

The funny thing is, after all of the raids we've experienced, this didn't really strike me as that big a deal. I just went along with my day. I went to the Korean grocery store for food (damn, $15 for a big bag of dried mushrooms), came home and cooked noodles, then packed up and went to GA.

There were tons of people there. We talked and talked, blah blah blah. The consensus of the physical Occupiers was to dig down and make it as hard to evict them as possible. They built new structures and asked friends to bring extra material. The idea was basically to make life hard on the authorities by piling as much stuff in the area as possible.

It turned out that the raid is most likely connected with the proposed meeting with the new sheriff. Apparently, he Tweeted us that he wouldn't be able to make the meeting himself and would send an assistant. Then we Tweeted that we had no interest in a meeting with anyone but him. He answered with the eviction notice. Basically we tried to play hard-ball and he decided to play back.

Didn't I just say how Monday was this big day? Well, here we are again.

12/16/11

I haven't written in two days and I'm way behind; things move fast around here. Yesterday I arrived on the scene around 10:00 am, which was when the eviction was scheduled. No cops were around, at least no more than usual. The place had really changed though. In 12 hours, both sides of the street had transformed from a line of tarps and blankets to a full-fledged shanty town.

There were hastily-built little buildings and random piles of crap people didn't want, like old fans and couches. There was a fully decorated Christmas tree, ribbon thrown through all of the trees, and spray paint on everything including the piles of snow left by snow plows. There was also a large, rowdy crowd of a hundred people or so.

The first order of business was to deal with money. All of our money was stuck in PayPal and you can't pay bail with PayPal! Tom had this cool idea that we could give him a PayPal gift of $2000 and then he could cash it because he's already got that cash. It seemed a little fishy that he's got two thousand dollars sitting around, but whatever. This went without a hitch and by 10:30 am, we finally had some money in our Credit Union account. That was an interesting experience; it's not every day that I'm running around with $2000 on my body, especially in that part of town!

I came back and saw that there was a big mic-check[9] going on. I quickly decided not to participate; "I'll just get a protest sign (there are always signs sitting around), plant myself on the street, and skip this discussion," I thought. As I attempted to tip-toe around the circle, I heard my name. Not a big deal, there are lots of Chrises in this world. Then I heard it again. "If you get arrested, call Chris." Hmmm, guess I'm not staying out of the fray after all.

Everyone looked at me and someone said, "Are you willing to NOT get arrested so we can call you?" This struck me as an odd question. Of course I'm willing to NOT get arrested! I even find the prospect preferable! And that started a process that took the next four or five hours where I learned far more than I ever thought I'd need to know about going to jail and paying bonds.

It turns out that to get your "one phone call" you have to call someone collect, even if it's not long-distance. This means you have to know someone with a landline. WTF, is this 1952? I checked around and no one at the occupation had a landline. One dude even asked me what a landline was. After several conversations with bondsmen, jail representatives, and internet-based third parties, I finally learned how to, and accomplished, setting up my cell phone to take such calls. The whole time I was thinking, "What does this have to do with activism?" But the fact is, yesterday, that's what activism looked like.

Around 11:00 am, a representative of the new Chief of Police came down to invite us to a Monday meeting with the Chief. He was quickly circled and harassed by a few members of the crowd despite Tom's attempts to keep things cordial. It's pretty funny when these folks try to use

---

[9] "Mic Check" has several applications in the Occupy world. In crowds it is used to get everyone's attention. You yell "mic check," everyone repeats it, quiets down, and proceeds to repeat everything you have to say. It's generally used for short announcements but occasionally can lead to impromptu soap box sessions. "Mic check" is also used as a noun, referring to these soap box sessions where people take turns telling a crowd whatever happens to be on their mind.

the People's Mic[10]. He didn't want to do it, but the crowd insisted. He kind-of went back and forth and often made his phrases too long to repeat.

I left, but heard later that while I was at home desperately getting a crash-course on the ins and outs of posting bail, the Chief himself arrived and received a similar response. This was all over the local press. Now we are deciding who will go to the meeting and what will be said and, like usual, the GA is taking it very seriously.

Here's an email I sent on the topic this morning:

"I don't know what happened last night at GA so this might be a little late, but here are my thoughts:

The idea of **recording the meeting**-this would be good for giving us the ability to demand consistency from the Chief, but I think it could be counter-productive. He wants a meeting so he can speak more freely. If we record the meeting, he'll have to treat it as a meeting with the press and measure his words and their political implications instead of just saying what's on his mind. I fail to see how that's useful.

Deciding on topics and delegates at GA-GA already decided to attend. The way I understood it, delegates would be decided upon by the individual committees, depending largely on individual schedules. I think debating and voting on delegates is a waste of time. Similarly, an open forum of discussion topics might be useful, but what is the point of a formal list of demands and complains? If this is a REAL conversation, it is going to proceed organically and the delegates need the freedom to improvise.

Overall-Ever since the eviction notice came, OD has been puffing up its chest and showing off its cock, but it's all bullshit. These guys can evict us when and how they want and every time the nightly news shows us being an uncontrollable mob, it gives the city more political leverage to do just that. It

---

[10] The People's Mic, is the practice of speaking in short statements, which are repeated by the crowd in call and response fashion. It's use became the norm in New York where they had enormous crowds at every GA but were not allowed to use sound equipment. Now it is used not only as a practical tool for amplifying one's voice, but also as a symbol of solidarity.

might not feel good to admit, but these guys are doing us a favor by having a meeting with us.

And all this internal negotiating over "should we go, who will go, and what will they say" is a distraction from actual activism. We should use the relationship between the 24/7 Committee and the mayor as a model. It's individuals having informal conversations where they actually discuss things and get to know each other. That's what actual negotiation looks like.

Meanwhile...the GA and its committees can get back to fighting political, social, economic, and environmental injustice. (Remember that stuff?)

Chris Mandel

That pretty much sums up my feelings of life in the Occupation in the last week and a half.

12/16/11 -B

Today was uncharacteristically quiet.

I was just thinking...what's the goal? I don't mean politically. We talk about that stuff all the time. I mean, what is the goal personally?

As long as I don't get income from the project, my current level of activity is unsustainable. Am I hoping we'll win and I can get back to life, only in a better world? Am I hoping that I can help the thing survive long enough that more people get involved and I can take a backseat? Am I going to get a career out of it? Is this even building my resume or my skill-set?

You know...there are probably unconscious or barely conscious motivations. All this work distracts from my problems; I'll bet that's one motivation. Another is that it makes me feel good to be working so hard on something fairly altruistic, something moral. Maybe I've got guilt about past actions and this is a way to make up for those things.

That having been said, I don't see anything particularly self-serving about my activism on the surface level. Yes, I'm gaining skills, but Occupy is so controversial that it doesn't generally look good on a resume. And any positive that might come from it is counteracted by the fact that it distracts me from doing anything else, even getting or holding a regular job or playing music.

Erin and I went to a jam session tonight and it was a lot of fun. It was my first large-scale free jazz jam in…wow, two years. That's a long time considering that used to be my life. It felt good. It was an open jam with a conductor who used hand signals to give basic commands. Despite how bad my chops are right now, I sounded good and felt at home. The conductors kept signaling for me to solo, which was super fun, but my endurance! My trumpet technique, especially endurance, is a shadow of where it is at my best. I miss being good.

12/17/11

It's Saturday. It's supposed to be my day off and when I spend time with Erin. But instead, I woke to a phone call from…let's see…it was Tom or Liberty, I forget. It turns out that someone got arrested last night for dumpster-diving. She was first charged with trespassing, but at her arraignment it was upgraded to aggravated burglary. WTF?

I'm not a conspiracy theorist and I always try to assume the best of people, but in this case I find it hard. Is this not an obvious case of harassing an Occupier with the intent of hurting the protest? By upgrading her charge, they justified giving her a high bail ($5000), which hurts us because it forced us to go through a bondswoman and spend $500.

Anyway, I ended up having about 20 phone calls over a period of three hours dealing with this and Erin was not pleased. Later tonight, she brought up the issue and said she felt left out of the decision for me to be so involved in the movement. Being involved was one thing but I'm putting in several dozen hours a week. What this means for my involvement and my marriage I'm not sure, but I do know that I need to start integrating my activism into the rest of my life in a more balanced fashion. It's tough, though.

I believe in what we are doing and I believe that this is my way of helping the world. I really believe this may be the most important thing I ever do with my life. I guess what I need to learn is that doing this activism, while it may be my top priority, it isn't my only priority.

And one can never forget to live a healthy lifestyle; it ultimately helps everything you do.

12/21/11

Let's see, today is Wednesday and our story begins on Monday. First I'll say that I purposefully avoided the occupation on Sunday and Monday, but heard a rumor that the meeting with Police Chief White didn't go so well. He said that all the encumbrances had to go, which isn't actually surprising.

It should be said that this guy has a reputation for firing bad cops and being reasonable. The occupation, on the other hand, does not have a reputation for being reasonable. They have a reputation for being incredibly self-righteous about their right to set-up tents and even wood shacks in the park and on the sidewalk.

The rumor was that a raid was coming on Monday night. I figured, "Hey, I've taken two days off, spent some quality time with Erin, gotten it together in other aspects of life…why not go down for the raid?" I wasn't in a hurry because raids (of which there's already been about five) generally happen late at night. But at 11:30 pm, Terese texted me: "You know there's a raid going on right now, right?" So I hastily packed up my car and rushed off around midnight.

Parking was tough. There were police everywhere and some of the streets were…ah. "When I Get Older" by K'naan is on Pandora. I love this song. Sad story though, the Chinese government heard it and loved it, so they contracted with K'naan to use it as the theme song for the Beijing Olympics. Then they actually listened to the lyrics and realized that it's about people's revolution. K'naan ended up changing the lyrics for the Olympics and putting out two versions of the song. It sucks; it's hard to not see this as a sell-out, but I really like the rapper and I want to see him as a revolutionary leader. Still, what's worse, K'naan changing his song or Ghandi beating his wife?

Anyway, I found parking a couple blocks away, next to the art museum on Broadway and walked up to the occupation. On 13th Street, just south of the park, was a mob of perhaps 60 pissed-off protesters and several dozen riot police, fully armed with batons, pepper-ball guns, armor, and masks. The police were in a long line, slowly pushing the protesters south, away from the park and towards my car.

In the background I could see bulldozers and smoke in the air. At the time I assumed this was tear gas, but I learned later it was due to the actions of some protesters. When the cops moved in, some young protesters started the shacks on fire, forcing the authorities to move in fast and deal with the flames.

There weren't many organizers there; it was mostly 24/7 Occupiers, half of whom are simply homeless people trying to survive. Roshan was there. Cory, Joe, and Anthony were present. Tanner had his camera. Christine and her partner from Occupy the Press were there too. There were also quite a few main-stream journalists running around. One of the first things I saw was Ben going absolutely berserk. He was yelling and trying to rush the police line as others pulled him back. I learned yesterday that his girlfriend Dana had been arrested a few minutes prior to my arrival.

Beside the protesters were two big tarps with random blankets and clothing on them. In the past, the police would confiscate everything. This time around, the protesters had managed to save some of their gear but the police line was moving forward and would soon overtake the position. I thought "I've got a car with an empty trunk" and I soon learned that some guy beside me did, too. So a handful of us pulled the tarps to the sidewalk.

They were big and heavy and it took three people each to move them. As we did, some of the police started jogging in a line beside us, presumably to circle the group. This caused everyone to start moving down road, some running. Pull, pull, pull!! We managed to drag the tarps across the icy sidewalk for about two blocks, almost to my car. I suggested that we put as much stuff as possible in my trunk but this grizzled old homeless guy said, "I don't even know you. How do I know I'll get my stuff back?" Good point, I hadn't thought of that. Instead, we pulled the tarps into a field next to the art museum. Fortunately it stayed there, safe all evening.

The cops continued with their strategy. They stayed in a line to keep us away from the park and occasionally made moves to circle us. I'd say this was a fear tactic. They were essentially threatening to circle and arrest the whole lot. In reality, if they really wanted that, they would have had a second group circle around in vehicles and trap us, but I don't think that was their plan. They just wanted the crowd to disperse while they arrested a few examples, which is exactly what happened. But not before we made a lot of noise.

One Denver PD cop came around the side in a cruiser. I don't know what he was thinking. He was alone and without fancy riot gear. The crowd was now in the middle of an intersection, slowing and stopping traffic. At this point, people started debating where to go. Some wanted to continue south to the Governor's Mansion, while others wanted to circle back around north to the 16th Street Pedestrian Mall. As this was debated (we even attempted to vote at one point), people noticed the lonely cop watching us.

Some folks went up to him to heckle him. This huge, young dude was super-pissed and looked like he was going to rush the officer. I grabbed him from the back and cried, "No, no, no! Come back to the group. We need you. We need you!" In comparison, I was a small bug on that guy's back. He had to weigh 300 pounds. So I gave up and watched. Unencumbered by my efforts, he was forced to choose: settle down or find himself in a battle with an armed cop. Sense descended on the young protester and while he continued to scream, he stopped moving forward.

After much debate, the group decided to move to a residential area. We headed east among the houses and apartment complexes. We screamed and chanted: "Wake-up Denver, Wake-up Denver!" "We are the 99%!" "Who's streets? Our streets." People watched from their homes and occasionally came out to talk or even join us. As we did this, we were followed by riot police standing on the outside of their trucks and a legion of cop cars with lights going. We eventually moved north to the major street, Colfax, due east of the Capitol and the occupation. We marched right down the middle or the road, slowing the traffic.

After a few minutes, a big truck came up from behind us. It was a semi with an open-topped trailer which contained all of our stuff! Presumably by coincidence, the truck carrying all of the confiscated belongings of the occupation had run into the leftover members of the protest. The vehicle was forced to slow and stop. A couple of protesters jumped in front of the truck and started Tebowing (prayerfully kneeling, named for the popular Bronco's quarterback).

Now I don't usually get involved in this stuff. I have agreements with Occupy Denver and with Erin that I won't get arrested. But this was just too perfect! I ran over in front of the truck and sat down in a meditative pose. I sat there and looked at the truck while one protester on each side of me continued to Tebow. Meanwhile, several other people jumped on top the truck and started pulling stuff out.

This lasted for perhaps three or four minutes. Then a long line of cop cars arrived. These weren't the same ones as before; these were fresh Denver PD guys. They showed up with maybe 20 cars and started pulling equipment from their trunks. It was time to go. I got up and ran. So did a lot of others.

Things settled down a bit but now we had twice as many cops following us. I stopped and stepped into a 7-11. I bought a soda and left. Now the cops were between me and the protest, which worried me a little. How would I get back to the group? Just then one of the trucks filled with riot police stopped at the 7-11. They passed me and went in, complaining that they were cold. I sat there frozen. I knew the safest thing would be to just leave but I couldn't. This was just too good!

I strolled back into the little store. Inside there were ten or so riot cops, still wearing their helmets and what-not. I went up to the candy section and picked up a Whatchamacallit. The officers were everywhere and it occurred to me that there would be no escape if there was trouble. I thought about talking to one, but that was pushing it too far. I couldn't do it. I bought my candy, pushed my way through the crowded stored and onto the street, which was now devoid of police and protesters alike.

I didn't meet up with the group again for about 45 minutes. I found them on the 16th Street Mall. The group was now down to roughly 20 people and the number of police was down, too. We continued down the mall making a loud ruckus; Gangsta Billy led the little troop with his booming voice and hand drum. I saw Ben get in the face of some policeman once again, but he was a bit more under control than before. Some big guy got arrested, maybe the same dude I'd tried to hold back an hour earlier. Oh, well. At one point, we were surrounded and another protester got arrested. Ok, that was enough; it was time for me to go. I slipped through the circle and walked as fast as I could from the scene.

I eventually found myself back at the park. It was empty and quiet. No protesters. No police. No fires or bulldozers. Just a park.

The next morning, yesterday, I woke to a phone call from Tom. It was time to deal with the aftermath. This isn't as easy as you might think. First you have to figure out who was arrested. You can get a list from the jail website, but it doesn't specifically list protesters; it just has names. We were attempting to put together a list but weren't done until I got a call from Ben. He had gone to the arraignments for everyone. We had nine arrested: eight for noncompliance with an order from a police officer and one for arson. First name on the list was Alex, a.k.a. Drew Kerry.

Ben said that the city lawyer pushed the judge to make the bail for all as high as possible because of their association with the occupation. He asked for $1000 bail each for the minor offenders. The judge set the bail at $550, saying that was the highest he could justify for such minor offences. The person arrested for arson had bail set at $50,000.

In the afternoon, I went with Ben and Tom to the headquarters of the Denver Anarchists Black Cross. They own a print shop in west Denver and have built a large center around the shop. It has a stage, a library, rooms for childcare and acupuncture. Things haven't been good with these guys lately. They went $8,000 in debt bailing Occupiers out of jail last month and have separated themselves from the movement, but in this case they had to make an exception because arson is cool!

I've got to say these young men and women have helped us a lot. They know WAY more about protesting than us, are more organized, and are better connected. We are super lucky to have had their support over the last three months, and personally, I'd like to see OD help them financially. At the meeting they were all super nice, and helpful.

That having been said, if you are a real revolutionary, you don't name your group the "Anarchists Black Cross." These guys idolize the labor activists of the early 20th century but I don't think they actually prioritize a *people's* revolution. The people don't like the word "anarchist." The people are either turned off or even scared off by terms like "black cross." From what I can tell, while they preach horizontalism, and bottom-up social change, they attract a small niche of white, well-educated, leftist intellectuals who are primarily on a mission to improve their individual hipster douche-bag credentials.

Case in point: halfway through our meeting, Ben had to take a phone call. It turned out that he had an interview with Keith Oberman, a nationally-known journalist and his assistant was calling to talk about logistics. Here we are, getting all this advice from these veteran activists, when one of the Occupiers has to stop to set up a high profile interview. My point is that these anarchists are cool and knowledgeable but Occupy Wall Street is the people's revolution. If DABC really wants to change the world, they would integrate themselves into the movement, not decide on a case-by-case basis whether Occupy is cool enough for them.[11]

Later that night, Tad brought the bail situation up to GA. By the evening we had eight of the nine out of jail. The remaining one has the arson charge and may be in for a while, unless the DABC can raise money for him. I made it home at about 11:00 pm, having done Occupy work all day. Now today I'm Occupying my computer.

---

[11] Through the editing phase of this book, the section about the Denver Anarchist Black Cross has troubled me more than any other section. As time went on, I learned more and more about the organization and anarchism. Many times I considered simply taking out this nasty analysis, not only because it's unfair to them, but also because it exposes my own naivety on the subject of anarchism and historical activism in general. Nevertheless, I've chosen to leave the section in. The analysis of the DABC might be unfair, but it's how I was feeling at the time.

What I now realize is that my basic critique, that the organization is intellectually elitist while claiming to be populist, is a very common problem for radical and progressive activists in general. I still believe the DABC is guilty, but so is Occupy, as are most progressive political organizations and movements.

Something else I didn't realize at the time I wrote this analysis was the importance of anarchism in today's activist circles, particularly in the Occupy movement. Many of the original organizers of the Occupy Wall Street action were anarchists, a number of the early organizers of Occupy Denver were anarchists, and most of the language and procedures of Occupy have anarchist roots.

1/1/12

There hasn't been much action lately; everyone's on vacation. I wrote a draft of the Declaration of Purpose today, here it is:

We are the subsection of the 99% of Denver citizens, who have woken from our slumber and cleared the fog from our eyes, to gaze with clear mind and open heart at the truth of our situation. We will not be pacified by commercial comforts or seduced by corrupt and/or ineffective political parties. With sober recognition we accept two facts: first, that despite the external appearance of a healthy society, this city is part of a nation which faces some of the biggest challenges of its short history. Secondly, that the current economic and political systems which shape our nation and our future have proven themselves to be ill-equipped to successfully meet these challenges. For these reasons, this system must be fundamentally reformed, rebuilt, and perhaps, reborn.

We dedicate ourselves to making Denver a beautiful, compassionate, just city. A city where the less fortunate are given realistic options for living meaningful lives. A city where all residents have affordable housing options. A city that prides itself on fair and effective criminal justice that authentically protects the freedom of the people while respecting the humanity of those who violate the law. A city that promotes responsible, creative business and investment and never sacrifices tomorrow's needs for today's wants.

We are also dedicated to major change on a national level. This country was founded under the principle that all people are equal and equally deserving of the opportunity to create a life for themselves. We feel that it is time to rededicate ourselves to this premise and deepen our commitment to its truth. In these 200 years of unprecedented individual expression, we have discovered that sometimes individual enthusiasm for lifting oneself up comes at the price of the good of others. We have also discovered that the structures we build for the good of human beings sometimes take on a life of their own and become parasites feeding on society and the Earth. In light of this hard-fought wisdom, we have come to the conclusion that just as our forefathers and foremothers courageously implemented new ideas, we must also.

Lastly, we the 99% of Denver acknowledge that the basic rights that we enjoy are not unique to citizens of the United States. All human beings, regardless of nationality, have innate value, beauty, and importance. They are not fodder for our own hungers or inconveniences to be dealt with, but potential sisters and brothers to cooperate with. Furthermore, all cultural expressions and societal norms demand a presumption of respect and equality, and cannot be judged as inadequate simply based on dissimilarity with our own ways of living. If there is suffering in the world, we have the right to help, but this can never be used as justification for economic or cultural domination.

We are living in a new millennium which presents new opportunities and new challenges. We are excited about this new era. We are optimistic about the changes presently taking hold. And we look forward to a better future, where individual opportunity exists in harmony with collective health and responsibility.

1/3/12

I went to GA last night. I don't have much to say, it was pretty normal. The main topic was about trolls on the Facebook page. Jason, one of our Facebook guys, asked GA for permission to kick people off of the page. Some people were concerned about censorship but by and large everyone understood and the proposal passed easily.

Afterwards, some guy had an "agenda item" where he went off about weird conspiracy stuff. CIA...JFK...I was hardly listening. He went on and on and on and on and on and on and on and on. Illuminati. UFOs. Chemtrails. On and on and on. Liberty was facilitating and repeatedly attempted to politely encourage him to wrap it up but his message was too important to be stifled. After twenty minutes of this, the most enlightening revelation of all finally came to light: "I know this is hard to believe, but OBAMA IS OSAMA," the young man said with a grave tone. "Compare their pictures...they look exactly the same." At this point Martin and I simultaneously turned away from the circle and busted up laughing.

The CNN Rule

Let me take this moment to explain the CNN rule. Simply put, ignore all theories about what's going on in the world that aren't mainstream enough to make it onto CNN. Don't base your activism on fringe theories; it's a waste of time. Don't get me wrong. It's possible that 9/11 was an inside job. It's possible that the moon landing was faked. It's possible that the pyramids were built by aliens. I'm not suggesting that fringe ideas like these are impossible or unintelligent; in fact I think it quite likely that some of these ideas have some truth to them.

In the past, I've been seduced by this stuff myself. I had a short Alex Jones/Info Wars phase and was really into UFOs for a while. I was even a paying member of Steve Greer's UFO website for several months. This was in 2005 or so. I had a friend who was into UFOs and talked about it lot. He played this famous NBC UFO program for me, which is very provocative and I walked away with an open mind on the subject. After that I read articles, watched YouTube movies, and listened to interviews on the subject constantly.

I remember the event that was the tipping point for me. A friend of mine, who's fairly mainstream and stable, told a story about a conversation he had with one of his high school teachers. This instructor had been, in a former career, a high ranking military officer. One day in class some punk jokingly asked the man if he knew anything about UFOs, and instead of laughing it off the teacher got very serious and sternly replied that there were certain things he wasn't allowed to talk about but that he could honestly say he knew things about the world that frightened him.

That night I woke up in the early morning shaking with panic. Aliens were real. Somehow this story, as told by my friend over a beer was the final piece of evidence; it was the tipping point. Aliens and UFOs became real for me, and as this idea seeped into my worldview a tidal wave of implications began to run through my mind. They could be involved in the government. They could be shaping our DNA. They could be monitoring, or even influencing my thoughts. I laid there for about an hour as these possibilities flowed uncontrollably through my mind. It was like a mental dam had broken. I wasn't trying to explore the implications of UFOs; they were running through my mind in a panicky, out of control fashion.

Then after an hour or two, it stopped. The world in which alien influence was a real possibility became my world, and after this short period of adjustment, I became at peace with it. "Aliens are real," I thought. "That's cool, whatever." I then went to sleep and never stressed about the issue again. Since then my opinion about UFOs has slowly shifted from "very likely" to "quite possible," but it's not a big deal. It doesn't matter. You can't know for sure about these mysterious things, nor can you mobilize around issues like these, so they just don't matter.

That night, when I put this particular issue to rest, was the first hint of what I would eventually call the CNN rule.

There are problems in the world; there are big problems in the world, and many of these are well-known in popular culture. The major, obvious, and incontrovertible problems with our world are so numerous and fundamentally important that we don't need supplemental, controversial theories to muck up the water. We don't need chem-trails from passing jets that spray brain washing substances; we can mobilize against conventional political propaganda and an elitist education system. We don't need George Bush purposefully causing 9/11. We can focus on the military, cultural, and economic imperialism of western states in the Middle East leading to fanatical antagonism on the part of local states, religions, and private military forces.

If a particular theory is too fringy to be reported in the mainstream media, like CNN, then you'll never be able to come to a consensus on the actual facts. If there is confusion about the facts, you'll never be able to mobilize mass resistance around it. It'll just never happen. Therefore, while the creation of alternatives to mainstream narratives is a perfectly legitimate intellectual endeavor, it is useless at best, and even potentially detrimental, to mass organizing. Stick to things happening on CNN; that's enough. The national debt is on CNN. The war in Afghanistan is on CNN. Global warming is on CNN. Bank bailouts, mass foreclosures, oil spills, the gap between the rich and poor, the failures of the healthcare system, the

American drug war causing poverty and strife in Latin America...all of this is on CNN and other mainstream news sources. There is plenty on CNN to get pissed off about; we don't need the extra stuff.

Let me be clear. I am not making an argument against grassroots news reporting; nor am I arguing that we shouldn't have open minds about fringe ideas. I'm saying that when it comes to mobilizing people into a political force, we should stick to popular, noncontroversial versions of the facts.

I mentioned Martin above. He is getting really involved these days. This successful, semi-retired IT professional, wrote a version of the Declaration of Purpose and is involved with an upcoming fundraising event (our first!). He will be playing the role of the President and will give a mock "State of the Union Address" during the real one given by President Obama in a few weeks. It should be fun!

One thing that concerns me right now is that Martin, Terese, and I appear to be all that's left of the Declaration of Purpose group. Terese doesn't really write and Martin and I have totally different visions for the document. How will we come to an agreement on ONE version? His style is very confrontational; he puts a lot of emphasis on making the motherfuckers pay! I'm the opposite. My version doesn't have one word about that kind of thing. I hope the presence of Terese will eventually help with this tension because I don't see how Martin and I could do it. We simply have different philosophies and there's no way to deal with it without one or both of us giving in on things we don't want to surrender.

While I'm really not down with the antagonism stuff, I might eventually have to deal with some going in. That kind of language is very popular in Occupy Denver and Martin is into it. Terese, thankfully, tends to have very similar views to me. "Thankfully." Look at all the ego that goes into this stuff; so much power struggle, even between friends and allies. How can it be avoided? We all care about this stuff and think it's important, and we all think, "I AM RIGHT!"

JANUARY

1/4/12

The occupation has been boring lately. There just isn't a lot to tell. One issue is that I've changed my personal strategy. I am doing less of the social stuff like protesting and showing up for GA and am instead doing more individual work. Namely, I'm working on an Occupy Wall Street PowerPoint presentation. I've probably mentioned it before. It is taking SO MUCH WORK! I can't believe it.

At one point, like three weeks ago, I thought "I'll just bang it out right now...maybe take three or four hours." Today I put in about four hours on one page! This is by far the hardest page to build but many have taken over an hour. There's research, finding pictures, editing pictures, basic design, animation, and keeping a separate page for notes and a bibliography. I can't believe how much time I've spent on it. I really, really, really, hope it is ultimately worth it. I've edited two movies for it and may do a third.

1/11/12

Again, not really much has been going on. The Finance Committee was audited a while back. Cory called for it apparently. It was kind of embarrassing; it felt like we were caught with our panties down, but ultimately I don't think it was a big deal. Neither Tad nor I is doing any real accounting. We have the records for the bank and PayPal obviously, but we aren't really keeping track of every little thing. That was Josh's role back in the day when we started the committee, but he starting occupying Boulder instead of Denver and we haven't replaced him.

Oh, wait. I've got an email to Roshan to send, I'll be back…Ok, I'm back.

We had a big meeting on the "Future of Occupy Denver" on Sunday. A lot of people were there, maybe 50 or so. The meeting was about seven hours long but I skipped out in the middle to go teach youth group. Actually youth group was the best part of the evening. No one showed up except for this 15 year old young woman who I'd never met before. We hung out for a while to see if anyone else would make it and it turned out she is an Occupier. She's not an organizer, but every Saturday she goes to the marches, which is pretty cool. It's nice to run into someone randomly like that.

1/15/12

I haven't gone to many Outreach meetings since that first one but the other day I went to present my PowerPoint. That didn't happen because we were so busy with other things, but at least there were some interesting conversations.

One of these was about what's left of the physical occupation. Marsha, a middle-aged, seemingly mild-mannered woman went off for about 15 minutes about the situation. She is involved with an effort to feed the group but is finding it very difficult practically and emotionally. The group is made up almost entirely of homeless folks, many of who have serious mental conditions or substance abuse problems. When anyone goes down to the Row, it is hard to find a stable person to work with and there are a lot of questions as to whether those people count as real Occupiers.

One side would say that the people in the Row don't understand the issues, rarely contribute to GA or any committee work, and would be on the street anyway, even if the movement had never been born. At one point

John went as far as to say that despite the continued presence of a little sleeping bag city, the physical occupation is essentially no more.

On the other side is a contingency that argues that the above statements are all based on prejudice toward the homeless. The homeless may not articulate politics well, but they feel its effects and are doing their best to represent themselves. Due to their various situations in life, they have limited abilities to participate in the more intellectual dimensions of the movement, but are nevertheless important participants. Albeit, on a purely physical level.

At one point, Roshan gave a little speech which I think summed up the situation well: the occupation started in late summer with a few middle-class activists moving into the park as a protest. This protest grew to involve several dozen full-time Occupiers, a few dozen more homebound organizers (such as myself), a few hundred part-timers, and quite a few homeless.

These homeless participants were primarily attracted to the food and relative safety of the encampment but many were also inspired by the politics as well. As the conditions got worse and worse due to the weather and increased police pressure, the middle-class Occupiers moved back inside, while many of the homeless stayed, having no where better to go. Now they have a small but strong community under the name of Occupy, but with dubious actual connection to the GA, which fancies itself the essence of the movement. So we've got two groups, barely connected, both with a strong identity as "Occupy" and both with a legitimate claim to that identity.

One solution that a few came up with at the Outreach meeting was to require certain things from Occupiers if they are to be fed. First on the list is to be sober. Second is to occasionally hold a protest sign. We'll see about that. Here's my opinion: it is up to the GA, not the homeless, to build this bridge. The general public sees the Row as the face of the movement, whether we like it or not. The GA must deal with it by putting some activists out there with pamphlets and protest signs. If the housed organizers are not willing to do that, we might as well abandon the park.

1/20/12

We seem to have a problem. Let me tell you about the Finance Committee. As I've said, it was started with five strangers, some of whom had relevant experience, some of whom did not. Over time, we have lost three members.

First to go was Dwayne. We had an on-site safe box which Dwayne was essentially in charge of. In one of police raids, all of our stuff was taken and we were no longer permitted any structures or large items. This meant no safe box. After that Dwayne, was essentially no longer part of the group and these days I rarely see his face at all.

Next was Willey. In the fall she was one of Occupy Denver's most active people. One day she was on several committees, the next day she was gone. She left an email saying she had to take care of her ailing father and hasn't shown her face since.

Last was Josh. He was always frustrated that he wasn't more included in the committee and eventually started Occupying in Boulder instead of Denver.

This left Tad and I, which was ok. The committee really doesn't do much and Tad knows what he's doing. In fact Tad has always done almost everything, including starting the co-op (which is our official legal entity) and the credit union account. When he started the credit union account, he got two cards, one in his name and one in Adrianne's name.

Well now here we are. I haven't seen Adrianne in a couple weeks (I heard she was sick), nor have I heard from Tad lately. Taking breaks is ok but NO ONE ELSE HAS ACCESS TO THE BANK ACCOUNT! I have passwords to the online stuff, but I do not have a bank card and I doubt that my name is on the account. If Tad doesn't show his face we have no access to the dough it contains. Fortunately, we don't have very much anyway, only about $500 in that account, and another $600 in PayPal.

And who looks like the inept asshole? I'd say, "Me." I'm the one who puts up with not having access. Erin is giving her Masters recital this weekend which means it's a wedding-like atmosphere with friends and family coming from three different states to see her. There is no way I can deal with this until next week which is, frankly, unacceptable, but that's how it is. I don't know what else to say; that's the situation.

1/23/12

I haven't been very involved the last few days but I plan on going to an Outreach meeting tonight. I still haven't presented my PowerPoint; that should happen tonight. I'm also working on organizing a house flyering campaign.

Oh, I should say what happened with the Finance situation. So I checked the accounts a couple days ago and found $360 missing. I didn't really suspect Tad of taking it. That would make no sense for a guy who's got a full-time job and has had access to far greater amounts of OD money many times. Nevertheless, I wanted to know what was going on so I texted him. He FINALLY replied to me, at which point I let him know that it was good to hear from him as I had feared the FBI had thrown him in a shark-infested volcano. I tell you, I am tired of this. I guess I should be upfront with him and say this to him.

Back to other topics. Something I've noticed within myself is a change in how I feel about telling people about my involvement. In the beginning, I was really proud. I felt like I was doing this great thing and that people should be proud of me and even thankful to me for being involved. And others had this attitude toward me. More than once I had people who weren't involved actually thank me for doing the work they weren't prepared to do.

Now it's different. I talk about my activism with a certain embarrassment. I'm not sure what this means. Part of it, I think, is the general reputation of the movement, i.e. we aren't beloved by everyone and even those who support us ideologically wonder about what we are actually doing. I guess my mixed feelings toward talking about it reflect my own questions about what we are doing.

It's not so much that I think we've done a bad job, but that there is already a feeling that we are yesterday's news. I think that in today's society we demand social phenomena to take place incredibly fast. Everything is done in sound bites and Twitter messages. Everything comes in quick tastes, and then we move on.

I really feel this pattern in music. I like to create music that slowly evolves. It starts in one place and takes its time to go to another place. But I find people don't appreciate that; most music gives you a short interesting sound, followed by another interesting sound, followed by another, and then it's done. It's just short back-to-back statements and then out. Each section is good, but undeveloped. There is no patience.

Anyway, we are only four months old. Movements take time. Organization takes time. But people don't see it that way. I'm afraid that the general belief is that if we were going to do something, we would have already done it. Or, in the case of my parents, the belief is that we already did do it. They argue that the goal is to be heard and force politicians and the media to take your point of view into account. Once this is done, they argue, you move on with your lives having succeeded in your mission.

When they told this to me, I thought, "So my friends and I are devoting our lives to this movement so that CNN gives us a 20-second blurb and Newt Gingrinch adds economic injustice to his list of talking points?" I don't like this idea very much. Of course my parents are not just thinking about politics, they are also thinking about me. They worried about what I'm going to do with my life.

I worry about this, too. I want to just devote my life to Occupy, but the job doesn't pay well. I assume that a lot of others are thinking exactly the same thing. How long will we put in countless hours for free? Frankly, in the long run, some people are going to start getting paid, while others will be forced to stop because the lifestyle is unsustainable. It's interesting. I think about this and think that positioning myself now, so that I'm one of those paid people, is important. But I don't like thinking that way. I'd rather stay pure, as an unpaid activist. The world of paid activist positions is a very gray area that often turns black. If you make money as a stockbroker, at least you aren't lying about your motivations.

You look at nonprofits and sometimes you see some ugly realities. When I moved to Colorado, I spent a few days as a paid canvasser for an environmental group loosely connected to Ralph Nader. I went door to door asking for money. If I made less than $100, I didn't get paid. If I made $100, I'd be paid about $75. If I brought in more, I'd get the base $75 plus 20%.

On your average day, the canvasser at the door would take home $85 or so. Where does the rest go? I had supervisors who had supervisors; these people got paid as well. At the top were state and federal lobbyists who, of course, got paid. Essentially, you, the good person who decides to give $100 when asked because you want to save the planet, have basically given the planet, maybe $1, and helped a bunch of other people put gas in their cars and TVs in their houses.

Here's another example: churches. Conservative churches will often justify their existence in terms of helping people be good and go to heaven instead of hell, but more middle of the road churches have different philosophies. If asked what they are doing for humanity, they will typically point to mission work and fund-raising efforts, and it's true, many churches raise large amounts of money for humanitarian efforts. But here are the questions: how much of that donated capital would have made it to those humanitarian efforts regardless of the involvement of the church, and does the extra money brought in offset the costs of running the church?

In other words, are churches truly helping humanitarian nonprofits by motivating potential donors and organizing fund-raising activities or ultimately competing with them for a finite amount of donation money? Is Habitat for Humanity better or worse for the efforts of the preacher who urges his church to give while he makes $50k a year? This is a difficult topic because I've known a lot of ministers and ministers in training who were honestly very passionate about humanitarian issues and were motivated to go into ministry due to these passions. But when I look at the actual economics of the situation, I don't like what I see.

What do you do? You want to help the world but you also want a home, and health insurance, and a retirement. As I write this, I realize that I'm not just contemplating an abstract social/economic topic; I'm discerning my future.

1/25/12

Ugg, my brain hurts. After a meeting I went to a bar with some Occupiers. Al was in a crappy mood and expressing it by buying full rounds of shots and PBR. I had three or four of these combos.

Afterward the two of us headed to his apartment to enjoy…some refreshments. Al is an electronic musician; he uses synthesizers to make dance music. We stayed up all night listening to and talking about music. This was the first time in many years I've done that and I can honestly say, probably the first time in over a year that I've been excited about music. I remember having nights like this all the time in college, as a music major.

Two days later and I still don't feel completely normal. I hate that feeling. Please go away. It's funny, the night was really fun but I'm left with a feeling that I'm getting kind-of old for this kind of thing.

1/30/12

In general, I always write this journal with an audience in mind. I've always imagined it being read some day but right now I just need to get my head around what I'm doing and what I need to work on.

My projects:

Flyering campaign. I'm trying to start an organized effort to flyer houses and street corners. I've heard someone else is working on this and that I should talk to him but no one has actually put me in contact with him.

Church Outreach. I built the PowerPoint presentation to use specifically with churches in mind but I haven't moved forward since finishing the presentation.

Finance Committee. This committee needs to be rebuilt. It also needs an official strategy for earmarked donations and expenditures, and needs to start doing some real accounting.

Declaration of Purpose. Can we just get it done?!

Occupation Journal (this book). Even in bad or boring times, I have to go forward with the project.

Last week, I went to an inter-committee meeting. I kind-of, accidently, went off about Tad in front of like 40 people. Oops. I really need to just talk things over with him. And we need to get one of the credit union cards in someone else's hands because the current set-up is dangerous. Both cardholders are marginal members of the movement at this point and could simply disappear.

I haven't done anything for Occupy in over a week; in fact, I haven't even been reading email. My energy isn't there. Consequently, all of these projects are on hold till I get it together. Hopefully just writing this journal entry marks a shift toward re-engagement.

Meanwhile, in other quarters, things are doing really well. We have a physical space to hold meetings in. It's a little community room above a local restaurant, near the occupation. We have about 20 active committees and working groups, many of which are doing quite well. Most GAs and inter-committee meetings have about 40 people. We're holding numerous teach-ins and outreach events, and we are starting to do some fund-raising, although we don't know what we're doing so the numbers are very small. I heard a rumor that the Mayor declared us dead, but I'd say he's misinformed.

The difficult part is watching the thing grow beyond my own involvement. I mean, being a big part of the movement used to simply mean showing up for lots of GAs. But we only hold two a week now and I actually don't go to any. It's all moving forward without me.

1/30/12

FFFFUUUUCCCCKKKKK!!!! My foot hurts. Outreach meetings are held a couple miles from the light rail station. On my way back, I skipped over a couple fences to shorten the trip. I should have known when I fell backward on my ass, as I jumped down the first time that this was a mistake. When I jumped down from the top of the second fence, I slipped on the edge of the curb and injured my right foot and ankle. Now it's 3:00 am and my foot is elevated and on ice. It fucking hurts!

2/1/12

For two days now I've been couch-ridden. My bruised right foot is wrapped with an Ace bandage and it's up on a pillow. Behind me are my newly-acquired crutches Erin bought for me. The other night, when I got home, she made an emergency trip to the drugstore at about 1:00 am for supplies.

Today I made about 20 phone calls to churches, attempting to schedule Occupy events.

It's weird, yesterday went great. I didn't have any outright "no's" and had several positive leads. At one point, I got a call back from a Unitarian Universalist church downtown. The guy called himself Wayne, listened to my spiel and then asked if I was one of the Chris's from Outreach. The dude had been at the very meeting I had attended the day before! I also talked to this guy, Rusty, who once interviewed me and decided not to hire me. That was a little uncomfortable, but he was somewhat receptive and passed my info to his justice and peace guy.

I spoke to the pastor at another UU church, this one in Golden, 10 miles west of central Denver. He said that a similar event had been planned in November but the organizer needed to reschedule due to sickness. Later the organizer canceled altogether and even bitched about the movement. It turns out this was the infamous Sarah F. who had the honor a few weeks ago of being the second person officially voted off the island by GA. She had been involved in the Wal-Mart controversy and had publicly denounced the movement on the internet. It's amazing what a disaster that 12/12 protest turned out to be.

Nathan and his community have some concerns about how peaceful Occupy is. Nevertheless, he was very enthusiastic about trying another event and we booked a date for a couple weeks from now. The sucky part…it's on a Sunday! I work on Sundays. So now I'm looking for people to fill a panel that I embarrassingly can't be part of.

2/3/12

Yesterday I got a text. The following is a transcript of my internal response:

Adrianne's back!!! Adrianne's back!!!

Adrianne, you will recall, has one of the bank cards, so her reemergence in the movement makes my stressy issues in Finance much easier to deal with. Now I've got someone with bank access who might answer my texts or emails!

Last night, my crutches and I made it to the weekly Spokes meeting[12]. Again I was on display for not having my shit together with Finance.

I did some soul-searching yesterday on this topic. I can't help but think that when I showed up to that first GA, I wasn't expecting to become an accountant. But you know what? We've got a planet to save and if the planet needs me to become an accountant, that's what I'll do.

Today I just finished this proposal; I'll probably bring it to GA next week:

Finance Earmarking Proposal

INTRO- This proposal is designed to create a system for donors to influence how their donations are spent by Occupy Denver, to promote fund-raising activities by individual committees, and promote financial transparency.

1) This proposed system is for all OD funds, other than any legal fund (which may or may not exist at the time of this proposal). Legal needs should be considered a separate issue from the rest of the OD budget.

2) Donors may designate what their donation be used for. They can do this by naming a committee or working group, a project, or event, or specific need. These earmarks must be specifically noted by the individual donor via memo line on a check, note on PayPal donation, or a written note with cash. Any donations with lack a note from the specific donor will go to the general fund.

---

[12] Spokes is the name of our weekly non-voting, internal meetings. In our case they are basically the same as GA, only we don't vote on anything. The name comes from other Occupations which use a unique system of "spokes" for organizing large numbers of people into a non-hierarchical, yet organized form. Each committee has a rotating representative in the inner circle who communicates with the representatives of other committees. This inner circle is surrounded by other committee members who may listen, but don't verbally participate. If need be, representatives can turn around and consult their committees or tag others to represent the group. Visually, the meeting looks a bit like a wheel with a small circle of representatives, each of whom is connected to a group physically behind them.

3) 25% of all donations will go to the general fund regardless of earmarking, unless the donor specifically indicates otherwise.

4) All earmarked donations will be associated with a committee and added to the appropriate committee fund. All capital, regardless of earmarking, will remain in ODs general bank account until a request for allocation is made by the GA or a committee. Committees do not need GA approval to request the allocation of capital in their committee fund. The separation of committee funds will be done internally by the Finance Committee.

5) All expenditures must be reported to Finance, preferably with receipts.

6) Finance will include a committee by committee breakdown of the current budget on the Administrative Committee's digests.

7) GA is the only body with authority over the general fund and retains ultimate control over the entire OD budget.

In day two of contacting churches, I had little luck. This led to two conclusions: first, I need help with this so I wrote a mass email fishing for people who want to start an official church sub-committee (if you just decided to give up on reading this book when I mentioned "sub-committee," I totally understand. I promise I'll get back to running from cops as soon as I can).

Secondly, I wrote up an email to send to churches. Normally I'd say the phone is better because it's more organic and human, but I suck at cold-call marketing, which is essentially what this is.

Here's my email:

Hi there,

I'm Christopher Mandel and I'm with the Outreach team of Occupy Denver. I am writing in regard to putting together an Occupy-oriented event for your community.

We have found that there are many church-goers in the Denver area who are interested in the Occupy movement and are passionate about the social issues the movement seeks to address, but are uncomfortable with or unable to participate in their local Occupy organization. Often these people simply want more information and a chance to ask questions and be heard in a safe environment.

At the same time, Occupy has often lacked strong voices from the church community, which in social movements of the past such as the labor, anti-war, and civil rights movements, often provided an important moral compass and sacred identity.

To build this bridge within our city, Occupy Denver has a church outreach campaign going on. We are putting together information sessions in local churches where Occupiers and church-goers can meet and share ideas.

This is an opportunity to cultivate understanding about the movement; ask questions of actual Occupiers who have lived in Civic Center Park; discuss the relevant issues such as economic injustice and corporate influence in the government; and address concerns about what has happened in the movement thus far and where it's going.

We would love to hold an event such as this at _____. How it looks can be shaped to the needs of your community. Weekends as well as weekdays are possible. Two hours is a good length but this is also very flexible.

If you'd prefer, we can also facilitate issue specific events (foreclosures, modern economics, or the history of American activism, for example). We can also send representatives to events you are already holding if this serves a need.

Please let me know how best we can cultivate a relationship that works for the_____community. Occupy Denver is here to serve the 99%. Feel free to call or email me; I'd love to have a conversation sometime.

2/4/12

Yesterday I sent out that email looking for people who want to be involved in church outreach and so far there appears to be a ton of interest and we may have quite a group.

I'm finding that working with people is challenging for me. While I can compromise and communicate with people pretty well, I find working with others emotionally challenging. Sometimes I'm so accommodating that working in groups is disempowering, while other times I find myself being domineering and feel self-conscious. I also get frustrated at the slow, inefficient nature of group work.

Nevertheless, I'm also learning that groups can motivate one another and hold each other accountable. It's a lot harder to drop a project when its initial luster wears off if there are a bunch of others depending on you doing your part. Plus, man, it is great to be able to suggest that something should happen and then someone else does it. That's just amazing. Apparently, the church outreach group will be born with me as a lead organizer. It's pretty exciting, actually.

2/5/12

Lots of OD stuff right now. I had time today, so I randomly went to a meeting about long-term planning and dreaming that Candace and Tom put together. Parking was terrible. I had to park a block south of the art museum, which is about three blocks from the Civic Center Park. I hobbled on my crutches past the museum, by the library, through the park, and finally arrived at the remnants of occupation. The group I was looking for wasn't there; I'd missed them.

I figured they had headed for the library so I turned around and pole vaulted back in the direction I'd just come from. I finally found the little group on the 4th floor. I'm so sore. My foot, my other foot, my wrists, and my armpits are all in pain. No more fence-hopping for me.

The meeting wasn't particularly noteworthy. There was a mix of active organizers like Roshan, Terese, and Candace, and several older people who are not very active in Occupy, but are serious activists. There was also Robert. I don't know him well but it doesn't take much time to develop an opinion as he knows how to make an impression.

We went around the room introducing ourselves and why we came. Robert took this as an opportunity to talk for about 20 minutes about…well, I don't know. I stopped listening. I know it involved fighting for cannabis rights and storming into someone's office only to get stopped by the secretary. I also know he started out his little speech by saying that he's highly skeptical about Occupy amounting to anything or getting anything accomplished.

Throughout the meeting, he kept jumping stack, getting off topic, and going on and on and on about things that I didn't care about. He mentioned several times that he despises the stack system, by which we take turns speaking. I quickly realized why he hates stacking. He hates it because it limits his ability to dominate conversations. Through the stack system, other people, even those too passive to interrupt, get a chance to speak. For someone who has no interest in respecting the rights of others to express themselves, stacking sucks.

I love the stack system. Since being introduced to the system, I've noticed that there are many informal occasions when I desperately want to take stack but it's not socially appropriate. Stacking has a major drawback: it makes quick response impossible so conversation has a stiff formality to it. I've observed that there is a threshold of about eight people where the benefits of the system outweigh the drawbacks.

If there are fewer than eight, it's better to use conventional conver-sation. At this number even those who are shy will generally be able to push through and get a chance to speak occasionally. But if there are more than eight people trying to communicate, there is always a breakdown. There will always be a couple people who dominate and others who silently soak in their frustration.

When you pay attention it's obvious; you can see it in their body language. They'll sit back in their chair while the dominant speakers lean forward. The speakers will have hardy laughs, while the passive only give polite chuckles. And I hate to say it, but there's a gender thing involved. The dominate voices will usually come from males. And as I look at the faces of the silent woman, I bet they're thinking, "These guys think they're so liberated and post-patriarchal but they still dismiss my voice when they're not thinking about it." And despite my occasional mixed feelings about the feminist discourse, I know that in this case, they're absolutely right.

As far as I'm concerned, stack isn't just for GA. Take stack in meetings. Take stack at the bar. Next time you go to a dog park and everyone is simultaneously barking, give each dog a number and explain that they have to take turns or else the expression of the less aggressive dogs will be oppressed.

I am currently working on the beginning of the book. I've put it off for weeks, but started to get worried recently that I was forgetting it all. I've written about 3000 words this weekend, all pertaining to the first few weeks of my involvement in the movement. It's fun to visit that stuff and see how far I've come.

Something clicked within me the last few days, I guess I mentioned it before. I am accepting that the finance of this organization is my responsibility. Like it or not, I'm the last person standing on Finance and no one new is stepping into the role. Hmmm…you know, that means I've got a pretty important role. If this thing is going to work, it needs me to do this.

That's pretty egotistical of me to say, but let me add that I'm not the only person in a situation like this. Admin now has only two members. Our internal regular newsletter has one person working on it. Occupy the Press, the main local Occupy journal, consists of two people. Legal also has two people.

This thing will be remembered as a movement of thousands, and they all matter, but some, due simply to luck, are in key irreplaceable positions and must perform or else the whole thing will fall apart.

2/6/12

I've Occupied all day. I worked on the beginning of this book for three hours; I went to Outreach, which is two hours plus commuting time; I traded emails with Matt in IT regarding starting an online store, and getting an email address for the church project; I traded emails with Cat regarding the co-op; I replied to an email from a church who wants to do an event (that's the second church to jump in!); and I corresponded with Blair from IT regarding the "99 Percent Foundation," which a number of OD people apparently started as a side project.

The funny thing is, here I am doing more OD writing. I'm just not interested in doing anything else right now. A few minutes ago, I decided to call it a night and play some video games. I couldn't do it; it was boring. Saving the world for real is so much more engaging than doing it in a game.

2/7/12

I'm having a good time with my involvement right now but I'm afraid I may be *too* involved. I just checked my money situation…not good. And spending all this time Occupying is dictated on not having much else to do, but the fact is, I can't remain under-employed forever.

Yesterday at the Outreach meeting, we decided to make the church campaign an open-ended, independent working group. This means it exists as a separate entity rather than a project within Outreach. It also means that I'm on four committees now and that's a lot.

Today I've been compiling a list of people interested in the church campaign and, thankfully, there's a bunch. I think there's a general feeling that churches represent an enormous, largely untapped resource. These organizations are morally motivated and interested in justice work. They are also organized, represent thousands of people in Denver alone, and have a status of social acceptability.

That last one is especially important. Occupy Denver has a mixed reputation. There are tons of people who dig what we're about but are uncomfortable with the counter-culture. Churches have the power to lend respectability. That which is associated with a church is automatically deemed safe and acceptable. This is absolutely crucial for going to the next level with this movement.

2/8/12

I just got back home from my first GA in three or four weeks. They are held indoors now and have quite a different vibe. I introduced the Church Working Group and later presented my Finance proposal. Cat, who was facilitating, made the mistake of believing that it would go through GA quickly and without controversy. She was wrong; quickly and without controversy isn't how the Occupy Denver GA rolls.

By and large, there was very little significant resistance, but Liberty and this fellow Lawrence were concerned about the idea of putting 25% of earmarked donations into the general fund because it could offend donors, so we took that out. There was also concern about the statement "The GA has ultimate control of the OD budget." The concern seemed to be that the GA shouldn't take from the individual committee's funds.

We took stack specifically on that issue and it went fine, until Robert came up. He stood up and began by saying, "This is so typical of Occupy. This provision is so obvious and debating is such a waste of time...." By the time he got this far I could no longer hear him well, but I know he was still talking because I could see his mouth moving.

First Cat held up a "point of process" hand signal, which means he's breaking the rules or getting off topic. Robert just kept talking. Then Paul, who came out of nowhere a couple weeks ago to become super active, yelled from across the room, "Sit down and shut up!" Robert kept talking. Then Anthony, who was standing right next to Robert, started screaming, "You always disrupt our meetings, you've got nothing good to say. Shut the fuck up!" Robert kept talking. All of the sudden ten or so people stood up, charged forward, and pulled Robert out of the room, all the while he continued to explain that the debate over the provision was pointless and that the GA was wasting it's time with the discussion.

We are the 99%. By now this is an overused cliché, but it has actual ramifications. If we were a conventional organization, Robert would simply be thrown out and told not to come back, but in Occupy we don't do that. Despite all of the unrest which has occurred in this movement, there have only been two cases of someone actually being asked to never come back.

Conflicts like what happened tonight with Robert are routine. It's nothing; it happens all the time. And I'll tell you a secret...I love it. I'm not a very dramatic person. I don't yell very often, I generally don't get angry at people. I haven't thrown a punch since I was 13. But as an observer, I'm a total drama junky! I just love the raw emotions and animalistic behavior that transpires in the movement from time to time. And to tell you the truth, as long as it doesn't get out of hand, I think it's healthy and natural.

I think these things are symptomatic not of a movement which is unenlightened, but of a movement that is unrepressed. Think of your average topics at a dinner party. Your typical board meeting. Your everyday interactions at the supermarket. Most classroom discussions. Do these things remain civil because they are mature or because they are boring? Are people polite because they have mastered their animal impulses or because those impulses have been put to sleep by daily activities which aren't worth waking up for?

I'm not advocating a world where throwing food at one another in disgust is the norm and cooperation is a rarity. But I think it would be a real mistake to dismiss a particular forum because of occasional strife; sometimes conflict is symptomatic of immaturity, but other times it is a sign of healthy passion.

On a different note, Roshan mentioned the other day that he's planning on dropping out of college due to money restraints. For a guy who Occupies for probably 40 hours a week, money restraints are linked with time restraints. He's dropping out because he doesn't want to pull back his activism for the sake of getting a full-time job.

I think about this and it's difficult to put the feeling in words. Roshan will probably never have a holiday named for him. He's most likely not going to win the Nobel Peace Prize or have a statue of his likeness standing in a public park someday. But he's making daily sacrifices to make this a better world. All of his classmates who have dedicated this time to developing their own skills and resumes move forward with their degrees and possibly lucrative careers, while he doesn't because he's decided that fighting for the needs of the country and globe is more important.

My friend Pat was recently written out of her family's will because of her political involvement. Nick at Night gave up on a normal housed life altogether so he could devote himself to living on the Row and organizing fulltime. You've also got people Erin, who isn't involved at all but has to put up with, and often times financially support, folks like me.

I just thought of something. I wrote a speech a few months ago that was never actually spoken and seems appropriate for this topic:

Mic-check. I'm supposed to come up to the People's Mic. And say that I'm pissed off about this. And I'm pissed off about that. But right now that would be a lie. The truth is that right now. I'm not pissed off at all. I'm fucking happy. I'm fucking joyful. Right now, everyday. I get the privilege of working with warriors. I get the privilege of working with heroes and heroines. Heroes and heroines who devote their lives to saving the world. Everyday I'm in a meeting. Or a GA. Or a protest. Or an email chain. With people I know are fucking saints. And every day I get up. And I drag myself to the bathroom. And I look in the mirror. And I think. Today, I have to try to be worthy. Of the company I keep. I have been given a great blessing. I have been given the privilege. To spend time. To work with. To become friends with. To become a brother to. Heroes. In one of her songs. Ani Defranco says. I have friends I haven't met yet. I have friends I'll never know. And I think about my friends. Far ahead of me in the march. Or across from me in GA. Or debating with me at a meeting. And I think about the 99% in Portland. In Detroit. In Boise. In Rome. In Hong Kong. And I look back at the mirror. And I think. These are my friends. These are my comrades. These are my sisters and brothers. And they are all heroes. Mic-check.

FEBRUARY

2/9/12

Yesterday I talked to Adrianne for about an hour. She explained how the relationship between the co-op and Occupy Denver works. Basically, the co-op is mostly under Tad's name which gives him a lot of responsibility. This is precarious given that we are dealing in conflict with the government. If OD was declared a terrorist organization, Tad would get the brunt of the legal response. This, understandably, isn't something he wants. I explained that when they disappeared, it left me afraid that the entire financial end of things was about to fall apart and we'd have to start over. She understood. What's funny is that I still haven't talked to Tad. But overall, it was a good step.

2/10/12

Yay, I had a meeting with Tad and Adrianne today! We met at the bank and signed me up on the co-op and bank account. Now I've got a bank card, which is a big step forward. We still need to start doing some real accounting though. I'm afraid we could get in trouble if we don't.

Last night we had the Spokes meeting. The most interesting part was at the end when we got in a big fight over what the last agenda item should be. Ever since we cut down our major meetings to two GAs and one inter-committee meeting a week, fitting in all the important agenda items has been a problem. Every meeting I've been to in this era (the last three or four weeks) has had agenda items tabled due to time constraints.

Last night we did an excellent job of managing time and got through about four agenda items within an hour and a half. Then it came down to 20 minutes and we had two agenda items: web issues and re-Occupying a park this spring. The later of these was tabled last week, as well. Roshan and Liberty argued passionately that talking about web communication was a more immediate issue and that re-Occupation was too big of a topic to cover in 20 minutes. Shaun and Tom argued that re-Occupation is more important than web communication and that the topic was being avoided, hence tabling it for two weeks in a row. We took a straw poll[13] and re-Occupation won out.

As we began the conversation, it became clear that this topic involves laws getting broken. In response to this, someone suggested that we shouldn't be having an open, public discussion about such a subject. This was the first time ever I'd volunteered to take notes. We take notes on most meetings and often post them on our website. I broke in with a "point of process" and suggested that due to the legal issues involved in re-occupying, perhaps we shouldn't post this section of the notes on the website.

This reopened the debate about whether we should be talking about re-occupation at all, which eventually culminated in Terese, who was facilitating, declaring that we needed to take stack on putting the notes on the web. This was with about 15 minutes left in the meeting and it should be noted that as part of our agreement with the owner of the venue, we have to be out by 9:15 pm with no exceptions. The whole room hated the idea of taking stack on the notes and finally the only way we could go forward was to switch to the other topic.

After the meeting, Terese made the observation that I've helped start conflicts at meetings twice this week (Robert and the Finance proposal being the other one). Nice.

2/13/12

I'm still on last Thursday. After the meeting, about half of us went to the bar. Given the state of my foot and the fact that I didn't have a car

---

[13] Formal voting is fairly time consuming and can only take place at official GAs, so "straw polls" are often done as a fast, informal way of getting a general idea of how a group feels about a particular topic.

available, there was no way for me to get home, so I went with Liberty in her Jeep and slept on her floor.

At her little house, I found five other Occupiers. Liberty took these former 24/7 Occupiers into her home, one by one, as winter got colder. Now every morning she wakes to four or five people sleeping in their living room. I'll bet that when she got involved in the Occupy movement, this isn't what she had in mind.

On Saturday, I went to my first protest in several weeks. At some point we got wind that there was a big fund-raiser for the Democratic Party. It was one of those events where, for a price, you can hobnob with big-timers in the party while eating a fancy meal. We passed out mock ballots which read, "No confidence in Democrats" checkbox, "No confidence in Republicans" checkbox, "No confidence in Obama" checkbox, and so on, and had people vote on what they have the least confidence in. Also, to symbolize the dinner aspect of the Democratic event, the Thunderdome came out and served food. The whole affair seemed more organized than our marches in the fall, but there was also dramatically lower attendance; only about 50 people showed up.

I didn't want to attempt parking downtown on a Saturday, so I took the light rail and the free 16th Street bus. On the bus, I found Drew Kerry with some of his friends. Drew Kerry was wearing his underwear on the outside of his pants and had stuffed them to appear rather noticeably excited. The whole time on the bus, he and his friends were loud and obnoxious and I kept thinking, "Are we going to have to bail you out tonight, Drew Kerry?"

At the protest it was a different story. Mr. Kerry and his little group were actually a very positive addition. They chanted, they sang, they danced, and they screamed slogans. Their crazy attitude, while inappropriate in a bus or just about anywhere in public, was a wonderful addition to the festivities of the protest. At one point, I found myself talking about it to John from Outreach. He mentioned that they made us look bad (and sometimes they certainly do). I said, "Yeah, but imagine how boring this protest would be if everyone acted like the two of us."

Later that night I got this email:

An open letter to Occupy Denver,
It's very disappointing that OD has chosen now to target the local
Democrats with the protest tonight. Just pure and plain sanctimony. OD
is just angry at everyone and everything. The OD folks can't recognize
possible friends or allies. OD is just against everyone and everything. I
donated to OD. I marched with OD. I delivered supplies to OD. Handed
out hand warmers. I spoke in support of OD to House District 8 Dems.
I'm not 100% happy with Obama. I hate the way Mayor Hancock and
Gov Hickenlooper have treated OD. We can change those sorts of
things, have made those sorts of changes, from within the Dems by
reaching out and letting our voices be heard. They do listen, really they
do, but after tonight, that's it, I'm done. They might listen a little more to
OD if they thought the group was anything more than a bunch of angry
sanctimonious blowhards. I've had my job cut 7 times in last 14 years - I
get it, we need real changes - but you'll need people to listen to you. Just
shouting and shouting will eventually lead to everyone just tuning you
out. If OD wants to oppose all organized politics, then great, good luck
with that, because after tonight - we're done with OD.

I responded:
Thanks for sending this email instead of just disappearing. If nothing
else, emails like this give the movement something important to think
about.

I'm extremely involved in the movement, in fact I'm basically devoting my
life to it, but I often see things transpire that I don't like. I remember one
of my first GA's when it was announced that the Denver occupation
was considered the angriest in the country. I expected the crowd to be
sad and apologetic but instead everyone was happy and proud. I didn't
understand how this could be considered a positive label and I still don't
like it. But I push on because I still believe this movement represents the
best opportunity for real healing we've seen in decades.

I participated in today's protest and I'm happy that OD did it. I thought it was a strong action. I voted for Obama and I don't regret it. I respect him and think he means the best. I actually consider him to be the best we can realistically expect in the White House. But nevertheless, the country and the world suffer. And that's the point.

This isn't about left vs. right; this is about the whole system being sick and inadequate. And at the center of that sickness is partisan politics and the economics that drives it. I have no doubt that that dinner in the Sheridan included good people who are potential allies and who honestly love their country and only mean the best. But this system, where people gain political access via their checkbook, is at the heart of the enemy. And by protesting an official Democratic event we send a powerful message to the political and corporate machinery, the media, the people, and to ourselves, that we will not be seduced into participating in the corrupt system. We are not protesting one side or the other, we are protesting the whole thing; and we demand a radical shift toward a more just system, which fairly represents average conservatives as well as liberals.

This having been said, I understand your frustration. Dedicating yourself to something, and then watching as it turns away from your values, or simply turns away from logical tactics isn't easy. I can only hope that if I reach the stage you've reached, I have the courage and compassionate to give a public explanation, just as you have.

He replied:
You sound like a pretty awesome person, and your reply is so incredibly refreshing. I wish I had your level of composure and grace. I'm not cut out for it like you are. When are you going to run for office?

If the movement was as level headed and focused as you sound, OD would have broader support. I really don't understand is the statement in OD's stand against the local Democrats efforts to fund their own grass roots - OD posted "we are engaging in a ruthless criticism of everything."

If OD is going to just criticize everything and do it ruthlessly, then what's the point? Tickets to the fundraiser were $150 to $10,000+, some could attend for 1% the level that others were paying. Most were not paying $10k - but that's all OD seemed to focus on.

OD seems angry at everyone and everything which doesn't seem to be in line with OWS:
-Engaging in direct and transparent participatory democracy;
-Exercising personal and collective responsibility;
-Recognizing individuals' inherent privilege and the influence it has on all interactions;
-Empowering one another against all forms of oppression;
-Redefining how labor is valued;
-The sanctity of individual privacy;
-The belief that education is human right; and
-Endeavoring to practice and support wide application of open source.

How many in OD are registered to vote? Obviously you are, but what about the rest? If they were paying attention, they'd be all set to show up to the Dem caucuses on March 6th. It would be great if OD members showed up to their own Dem caucuses to help encourage change from within. Details on locations and the caucus process are at www.denverdems.org. Encourage them to stand up and run for Precinct Committee Person, run for delegate to the county and state caucus.

Direct democracy is participating in the process. Unless OD plans on a revolution, change will have to come from support within and by elected officials. I dedicate my time to getting out the vote of people who share my views - canvassing hundreds of homes and hundreds of phone calls to get support for health insurance reform - volunteering in campaigns of candidates that support things I care about. I'd much rather have a single payer system, but that's not on the table, yet! How would OD members have liked Ken Buck for Colorado senator - we put time and effort to do everything possible to keep that nightmare from happening. Is Bennett perfect, not by far, but many of us continue to let him know where we stand on the issues he's facing in the monument to Murphy's law, the US Senate.

I'm not happy with the Denver mayor, didn't vote for him, didn't support him. But I did write him and others in the city to let them know how I felt about treatment of OD. If a few thousand, tens of thousands others can join in, they pay attention. Constantly shouting a "ruthless criticism of everything" will fall on deaf ears.

I hope OD can work through the growing pains. Good luck.

I think this fellow has a good point but also makes a fatal mistake. He has a point that the Occupy movement needs to start strategizing about concrete ways to change things. Just yelling all the time does little to nothing. But he makes the mistakes of believing in the status quo system, and reducing politics down to partisan struggle.

He believes that the system can be reformed from within. All of the evidence points to the contrary. How often has the system successfully made self-regulating shifts to significantly make the machine run smoother and more efficiently? The history of movements engaging in the system is a history of powerless third parties and movements becoming impotent after being co-opted by large political forces.

This makes fundamental change very difficult. We don't have the power for a full-scale revolution and, even if we did, violent resolutions rarely culminate in resulting systems which are superior to the former systems. So you say, work from within. Elect candidates. Pass ballot measures. But it is this system which is corrupt and incapable for real reform. The result of this paradox is a movement which does nothing but scream about its anger. I don't have the answers. I don't know how to address this paradox. But I do know that continuing to push is the first step. Going back home and giving up out of frustration or exacerbation will not save this world; we need to keep pushing and hope that a strategy emerges.

2/14/12

Last night I met up with Jason at an Occupy DU meeting. We talked a bit about the 99 Percent Foundation. It's a non-profit started by a number of current and former Occupy Denver organizers. He said it is envisioned basically as a more legal and acceptable organization than OD. It is designed to attract major contributors. What I find strange about it is that most people involved in OD don't know about it. It has been formed almost as a secret, although I'm sure the founders wouldn't say that. I later talked to John about it and suggested that it's a potential competitor. John disagreed and said its function is different. It's an independent, more mainstream arm of the Occupy movement in Denver.

Later that night, I got wind that Matt and his girlfriend Kylie are no longer participants. They separated themselves from the movement for some reason a few weeks ago. This news tore me up and I had to stop and ponder why I was taking it so hard. When I first started, they were central figures in the movement. They are young and energetic and were super passionate about activism. They had a wonderful balance of 75% seriousness and businesslike attitude with 25% Drew Kerry-like craziness. Once in December we Occupied a dance club together.

It's weird to hear that they are gone. Strategically speaking, I don't actually remember what the two of them did in Occupy but I know it was something. They participated in GA all the time and I think they were involved in the 24/7 Committee. Kylie was on Admin perhaps? The movement is the people and every time we lose committed people, we grow weaker. So many of our committees are complaining that they need more members and this is why. We form these committees, people leave, and then you've got a committee trying to perform its duty with a fraction of the people who formed it. And something I've noticed is that new people don't always want to join old committees; they'd rather start new projects. This leaves older groups, which are generally more fundamental to operations, starved for bodies.

Sometimes Occupy Denver feels like a combat zone. One moment you're working side by side with people, building relationships as you go, and the next moment they are just gone and you never see them again. Relationships don't usually end that way. Usually the people you know slowly fade from your life, easing the pain of disconnect, but not in Occupy. It's either in or out. Some people, Tad for example, slowly pull back their involvement, but more often, people just get fed up and disappear. It's like we are teenagers hanging out on a Saturday night in haunted mansion. One moment you're playing an innocent game of "truth or dare," and the next moment someone is losing their head in the bathroom.

It gives me this vague nervous feeling. Who gets axed next? I hear Liberty is super-stressed these days, and who can blame her with all those Occupiers sleeping on her floor? Is the axe murderer going after her? I also hear Roshan has decided he is going back to school next term. Is the axe going to come down on his head?

In a couple months is GA going to consist of myself, Cory, Robert, and Drew Kerry? Or perhaps the axe murderer has his evil bloodlust focused on me.

2/17/12

The day after I wrote about Matt and Kylie leaving, guess who showed up at GA? I talked to them a bit after the meeting and it sounds like they've been going though some major upheaval for the last couple of months. They've been kicked out of a house or something, Kylie's mom passed away, they are at war with their relatives, and don't have any money despite being employed. So the whole story about them quitting in a huff may not be true.

2/18/12

As I've mentioned in the past, this is my first major foray into activism. I've always wanted to be more involved in social change, and have flirted with it a few times, but this is my first experience with really diving in.

Up until now, my life has been about art (particularly music) and spirituality. My thesis in graduate school honed in on one of my greatest passions: esoteric jazz music. Specifically, I studied the spiritual lives of avant-garde jazz musicians and how that spirituality related to their music. While I had always felt a deep connection between the music and my own spiritual life, and was aware of a wide-spread connection that dates all the way back to the first days of the genre in the early 60's, I was nevertheless surprised when almost every musician in the genre I talked to, regardless of whether I previously thought of them as spiritually inclined or not, had an active spiritual life and felt that it was intimately connected it to their art. I ultimately concluded that despite secular marketing, avant-garde jazz is essentially a sacred form of music.

Now I've all but given up playing music and have little interest in metaphysical speculation. I still meditate on a regular basis (generally at least a few minutes and sometimes up to two hours a day), but it basically stays in the confines of the practice itself. I no longer obsess over the nature of the universe or the relationship between my ego and the external world or similar topics. Ten or twenty years ago I might have stayed up all night, lying in bed contemplating free will, supernatural phenomena, or the nature of right and wrong. Now I contemplate 501(c) status, consensus voting, and website design. My mental energy is dedicated toward accounting methods, the difference between committees and working groups, and the strengths and weaknesses of cold-calls versus emails.

These days I am obsessed with organizing. I have always seen my generation as a herd of cats. Individually, they are politically motivated, but they have no capacity for creating lasting social structures. This synopsis came from my experience in music, where over and over, I saw musicians come together in a common mission only to break apart after a few months because the group mission never transcended individual agendas.

Occupy is the first time I've ever experienced meaningful group identity. It's the first time I've ever seen people persistently put away their individual agendas to further a group cause, and day by day by day it challenges and inspires me. Hence I am obsessed, not with politics, or fighting cops, but with the process of organizing.

I recently realized that the avant-garde, mysticism, and activism have something in common, deep in each of their cores: all three are attempts to throw off the shackles that limit our freedom and the quality of our lives.

The avant-garde sheds the limitations inherent to conventional ascetics. Your typical music fan isn't aware of it, but our common standards of artistic beauty, marketability, and artistic legitimacy are a tightly interwoven matrix of rules that dictate that the musician shall avoid 99% of the sonic possibilities at their disposal. And if an artist chooses to break these rules, they are severely punished monetarily and socially. We often see these artists as losers among losers. They are labeled as both professionally unsuccessful and elitist snobs. They are simultaneously seen as below the mainstream (the deadbeat, lazy artist) and resented for being above it (the stuck-up, self-righteous hipster).

On the extreme end, this resistance can even be violent. Famously, the premiere of "the Rite of Spring" by Igor Stravinsky literally caused a riot. Not a metaphorical riot, an actual riot. And in his early years in the jazz and R&B scenes of Los Angeles, Ornette Colman would periodically get kicked off the stage, pulled out of the bar, and beaten up.

The avant-gardist looks in the eyes of this oppression, and as he or she screams on a sax, writes atonal notes on a sheet of paper, or creates feedback with a guitar, they are telling the world and its ideas about acceptable musical statements where to go: the music industry can go fuck itself. Mainstream ascetics can go fuck itself. The conventional standards of professional success can go fuck themselves.

I can speak from experience of the effect that this emancipation has on your soul. You are, quite simply, filled with joy. And despite what may sound on the surface like anger or torture, the music is really music of happiness or even bliss. When you make the jump out of conventional genre, you pay a price: people leave your show in the middle; your family thinks you're a loser; and venues refuse to book you. But in the heat of the moment while playing, you feel like a freed slave. It's like, "I don't know where the next meal will come from, but I'd rather be hungry under the stars, then sitting in a cage with a full stomach."

Mysticism. It's interesting. Religion actually does two totally contradictory things at the same time. On one hand it can be an institution which socializes people into conventional worldviews and lifestyles. This is both good and bad. It can pull up those living "below" the conventional by helping young people, the homeless, the drug addicted, and those in prison. But it can also hold back those who would otherwise go beyond the conventional ego-driven, consumer worldview. Good churches do more of the former while bad churches concentrate on the latter.

Ironically, religion is also the seat of most mysticism, which is the opposite of socialization into the norm. The spiritual seeker has realized that something is terribly wrong with the world and while they might not understand what that thing is, they know where it is. It is inside your own mind.

A prerequisite to serious spiritual practice is having a hunch that you have been sold a lie. You must cast off your assumptions. You must question everything you take for granted and challenge every precept which has been handed to you. The hope is that when this is done, you will gaze at reality as it really is, and in doing so become free of the shackles of illusion. While spirituality often involves intense training and adherence to a strict way of living, at its heart it is about shedding limitations rather than staying within them. It is about shedding the limitations associated with the separate, ego-driven identity and the cultural baggage which promotes obsessively self-interested living.

Lastly is social activism. Activism is about freedom in two ways. First, activism is about helping the oppressed. Sometimes the oppressed are a tiny minority, other times the oppressed group is the vast majority. But in all cases true activism involves empowering the less fortunate.

The second, more subtle, emancipation involved in activism is for the activists themselves, regardless of where they are in the social hierarchy. Through the activity of social/political involvement itself, the activist is freed from their own instincts for self-serving activities. Along this path activists let go of other weights pulling them down. They forget their fear of association with less fortunate populations; they let go of their need to follow the rules of normal public behavior; and they may even lose their fear of incarceration.

Even in the case of an oppressed person fighting for their own rights, they are risking serious repercussions; there is almost always a certain self-sacrificing quality to activism. And like the emancipated artist, or the freed soul, the experience of overcoming fear and simply doing what's right is immediately gratifying. It is its own reward. It is freedom itself, even before that freedom is reflected in the external world.

In this way mysticism, activism, and the avant-garde musician or artist, are very similar. They have all grown fed up with the status quo and its inherent limitations. In response, they have chosen to throw off those shackles, live in a more authentic and free manner, and deal with the various consequences which may come as a result.

2/20/12

A couple days ago we had the first ever Inter-Occupy Colorado event. About 150 Occupiers from around the state gathered in the physics building at CU Boulder from about 9:00 in the morning until 6:00 in the evening. This event, organized by the 99 Percent Foundation and Occupy Boulder, was structured like a convention, with small topical breakout sessions followed by a long meeting with everyone present.

I arrived a little late and missed the opening breakfast, but made it to the first breakout session. I choose to go to "Economic Inequality." It was led by a woman from the CPC which stands for... well I don't really know. Colorado Poverty Clinic? Whatever.[14] In any case, she explained that she's been an activist for a long time and that CPC was super excited about the Occupy movement. They are currently working on putting a measure on the Colorado ballot regarding changing the state income tax to favor the poor instead of the rich.

Next I went to "Movement Building." John put this together last-minute when he realized there weren't any sessions planed regarding outreach. He asked me to mention the church outreach I'm involved with but that didn't really happen. There were several cool ideas though. Someone mentioned organizing an Occupy movie night where you show relevant films. Cool idea, let's do it!!

The conversation in the session kept getting side-tracked. At one point Tom got in a debate with this guy who looked like Dumbledore and was from the little hippy town Nederland. They were arguing about working within the system, and having specific demands, and using non-violent tactics ....Oh sorry, I fell asleep there for a moment. I've heard

---

[14] Colorado Progressive Coalition

debates like this a time or two in the last few months. Despite the tangents it was a good session.

Then we all gathered in a big session to discuss cooperation between the Colorado occupations. The first topic was the upcoming May 1st strike. Occupy Denver has been working on this for a couple weeks and I've heard GA discussions on the topic on three separate occasions already. I was really tired because I hadn't slept well the night before, so I slipped out and found a bench to sleep on. 20 minutes later I went back in. They were still talking about May Day and were about 20 deep on stack. I went back outside.

After another 15 minute nap I crept back into the large classroom and found that stack was on 30 now! Still May Day! At this point I figured out the problem. Jason was facilitating. He's a smart guy who works on our Facebook and helped started the 99 Percent Foundation. He was facilitating because he helped organize the event, but he has little experience facilitating and here he was trying to orchestrate a conversation between 150 people. Despite all of his talents, this was beyond his skill set. Terese or Roshan would have moved on to other topics long ago, but herding cats takes practice; Jason doesn't have that practice yet.

Perhaps the most interesting part was when one of the organizers from Boulder, Lee, broke down the festivities for after the convention. Occupy Boulder had put a lot of energy into organizing a march, and finding a space downtown for an all-night occupation. They had a tent and food, and spent several hundred dollars on permits.

These permits, Lee explained, came (as permits generally do) with rules. No sleeping, no closed tents (meaning tarps and canopies are ok), no excessive noise, and no absolutely NO drugs or alcohol. Lee said that Occupy Boulder expected these rules to be respected.

Did I mention that Cory was there?

Cory raised his hand and said that there was no way he would comply with a rule against smoking pot. Lee squirmed and a dozen hands shot up to go on stack. Most people were on Lee's side but a few supported Cory's point of view. I spoke up and said that I considered myself a guest of Occupy Boulder and I'd comply with their requests. I got a little ovation for that…I'm so special. The conversation pretty much ended there.

Most people left, tired after a seven-hour convention and wanting to head back to their hometown. More probably would have stayed but hey, no closed-walled tents? How were we going to party all night with no tents, no sleeping bags, no noise, and no drugs?

By the time the march began we were down to about 30 people. The Boulderites had originally planned on going through the University of Colorado campus, then down the sidewalk of Broadway to the Pearl Street Mall and finally to the courthouse, where we had a permit. But by now the Denverites and a couple of the more hardcore folks from other towns were getting fed up with the law-abiding ways of the Boulder organizers.

It was agreed upon that you can't chant, "Who's streets? Our streets!" from a sidewalk. Instead we'd go through the middle of Broadway.

Now, I realize this journal has already included several marches and I totally understand if they are starting to blur together and lose their sex appeal, but there was something special about this march. Maybe it was because it was so small; only 30 people. Or maybe it was because it was essentially impromptu rather than a big affair planned weeks in advance. I'm not sure. But strolling down the middle of Broadway, the busiest road in town, stopping north-bound traffic for 20 minutes was amazing. A big flag and a couple banners appeared out of nowhere, as did Tanner's beloved bullhorn. I was still limping a bit due to my injury a few weeks ago, but felt great singing and chanting as cars behind us desperately honked and attempted to pass.

"Who's streets? Our streets!" I've cried this dozens of times and never thought about it before. But as we crossed Canyon, ignoring a red light, I felt the meaning of the chant. We generally obey traffic laws because those are good laws that make our society safe and transportation fast. But let us not forget, these are our streets! If we choose to ignore the rules for a while, that's our business. We have the right to, because they are our fucking streets and we'll do what we please!

We went to the park and it was the funniest thing. All of the energy just evaporated. The food wasn't there yet, there weren't many people around, it was cold, we couldn't camp or get drunk, and one more little thing.

There were no cops. The whole evening, there were no police officers.

I mean, when we decided to pull out the bullhorn and walk down the middle of Broadway there was a collective, unspoken understanding: we were stirring things up. This was going to lead to a confrontation and possibly arrests. Frankly speaking, that was the plan.

Where's the riot gear? Why don't we hear sirens? We kept thinking these things as we marched.

"How," the poor Occupy Denverites thought, "are you supposed to have a protest without cops?" "Who are we going to yell at?" "Who will we complain about afterward?" "What will Cat [our primary legal person] do tomorrow if there's no one to bail out of jail?"

Soon Occupying the courthouse led to Occupying the bar.

2/23/12

Today began with an Occupy event, then afterward I went to an Occupy event, and after that I thought I'd unwind a little, so I went to an Occupy event.

First was the teach-in on nonviolence. As far as I was concerned, I was scheduled to present a short presentation. This was my first ever presentation or speech in Occupy and I was excited about it, although a little suspicious it might not actually happen. I prepared material about neurotheology and its ramification for non-violence.

I was in the car, driving to the venue and was thinking about brain science and its implications for non-violent behavior when I realized I was going to be late.

My thoughts during this 15 minute drive:

Negative feelings are seated in the ancient limbic system of the brain. *Why did I leave so late?!* Those uniquely human qualities like compassion and reason emerge in the neo-cortex, the outer layer of the brain. *What the fuck, why are there so many cars on the road?!* Good moral judgment happens when the neo-cortex is firing and the limbic system is quiet. *Get the fuck out of the way, I'm in a hurry!* Learning to control one's mental habits is necessary for remaining calm in stressful situations. *I'll just drive in the bus lane for a while.* Training one's mind is no different than training the body, it just takes practice. *Jesus, now I have to park. This sucks!* Once you master the mind, which is no different than mastering any other biological function, you are no longer slave to your thoughts and emotions. *Yes, finally, got a spot. Run, run, run!*

I eventually got there and made my way up stairs. I hadn't missed much, and it wasn't a big deal since I quickly found out that too many presenters had been booked and I wouldn't be speaking after all.

First up was this older fellow. He went off about non-violence or something for like 20 minutes, then the main organizer, politely told him he needed to wrap it up because there were other presenters. The gray-haired professor continued on, with a comment under his breath "well others will have to wait." He went on for another 15 minutes.

I kept thinking about my enraged drive up from southern Denver, and how it's funny when people talk about morality and non-violence, while acting selfish or out of control. Here's this guy going off about the merits of love and compassion, but he's putting himself ahead of others who want to speak and the audience in general. He's talking about equality and non-hierarchical structures, and taking up 40 minutes of a 2 hour round-table meeting talking about it. Later, when others were speaking, he raised his hand over and over to make long comments. Obviously in this world of equals, he's the most equal of us all.

I don't mean to put him specifically on the spot; the group, as whole, did the same thing. As we discussed respecting others, we went over by 10 minutes, forcing the next group in the space to start late.

Next on the docket, starting 15 minutes late, was spokes council. The most interesting part was near the end when we talked about Moveon.org. I don't really know much about this group, or the situation, but what I could gather was apparently they are a liberal group which emerged in the 90's in defense of President Clinton during his big sex scandal. Since then, they've been a very active, proudly democratic, organization. The important part here is that unlike Occupy, they are overtly partisan, openly backing the Democratic Party.

Lately they have been involved in the "99 Percent Spring," which is pushing...I don't know... it is pushing something. The important part is that they are essentially trying to co-opt the movement on part of the Democratic Party. They are using the language of Occupy but aren't actually affiliated with an organized Occupation, nor are they non-partisan or particularly radical.

So several Occupiers have been getting emails from Moveon, offering to cohost events and whatnot. It's a pretty obvious attempt to associate themselves in the public eye with Occupy. At spokes there was a heated debate regarding this issue. One side said that we should make allies wherever we can, we need to cooperate more with other organizations, and we can get along on specific issues and at specific events without officially endorsing Moveon in whole. This group, led by Roshan, suggested that we are just as likely to steal their members as they are to steal ours and that through cooperation, we might be able to influence them.

The other point of view, expressed largely by Tanner, said, "Fuck Moveon.org!" Spokes found their point to be well thought out, eloquently put, and ultimately convincing. Moveon.org will not be worked with.

After spokes, there was a meeting at our usual bar for the upcoming May Day strike. To be honest, I didn't really hear it as, "May Day meeting at Santa Fe Bar and Grill." I heard "everyone to Santa Fe Bar and Grill, maybe we'll talk about May Day." So Candice and I enthusiastically headed down to the restaurant.

Once there, my slight misunderstanding of the meaning of the meeting became relevant. At first everything was fine, fun was had, Candice even bought me a beer, and everything was going great. But after a few minutes we got down to business and started discussing the event. We even took stack! "Wait a minute here," I thought. "What am I getting into? You tricked me!" Soon I found myself committing to being involved. Damn it, another project. All I wanted was a beer!

2/26/12

On Friday, a group of eight people locked themselves in Tom's living room with the singular mission to finish the Declaration of Purpose. One little delight was to see Wiley there. You'll remember that she was an original member on Finance. She also founded the Non-Violence Committee and helped form the survey which launched the DOP project. Due to an illness in her family, she went several months without showing her face but I thought, since she helped start the project, maybe she'd be interested in helping to finish it. I emailed her, and to my surprise there she was in Tom's kitchen when I arrived.

We began by discussing our audience and strategy for the day. It was decided that we'd take Tom's most recent version as a template and go from there.

Wow, what a tedious process. We began at the beginning of the document. An hour later we had the first sentence done. We then went to the next sentence. Over the next seven hours, we went paragraph by paragraph, sentence by sentence, and word by frickin' word discussing and debating how the document should go.

Here are some examples of contentious issues:

- To capitalize "P" in "the people." We eventually agreed on a temporary fix: ℙeople
- "Workers" versus "people." Some liked "workers" but others felt it was too blatantly Marxist.
- To use the phrase "We are the multitude." This led to checking the history of the term on Wikipedia, which then led to a discussion about the politics of Baruch Spinoza.
- To use the phrase "life, liberty, and the pursuit of happiness." Some felt that quoting the Declaration of Independence makes the false assumption that everyone in OD supports the continued use of the document. Others thought using the phrase was an important way to connect to the history of the USA and bring in mainline Americans who believe in constitutional values.

There were times when we disagreed about long versus short sentences. There were long discussions regarding punctuation. Ultimately we gave up at 7:30 pm, having completed about 40% of the document.

MARCH

Son, sit down, get some hot chocolate, and let me tell you the story of the "Fuck the Police" march.

Thursday:

For several weeks there have been rumors of a FTP march being held this weekend. I first got wind of the controversy surrounding it at the non-violence teach-in. While not actually being an organizer for the event, Cat stood up and represented it. She explained the tactic of "black bloc" and talked about the Denver Anarchist Black Cross which didn't organize this particular march either, but had been involved in similar events. A black bloc is where anonymous, masked protesters, wearing black, walk with locked arms down the middle of the street. This, as you can imagine, is often met with police resistance and fear on the part of ordinary residents. It seemed strange to me but when explained by Cat it made more sense. Funny how people usually make more sense when you take the time to listen to them.

This culminated in a lot of attacks by the non-violence crowd regarding the name, "Fuck the Police." All Cat could really do was remind them that she didn't have anything to do with organizing the march.

Friday:

After we put away the Declaration of Purpose, those still at Tom's house discussed the upcoming march. It turned out that the WestWord was telling people FTP was an Occupy Denver event. Tom talked to them and emphatically told them it was never passed by GA and is not endorsed or organized by OD. Later, the WestWord quoted Tom as having claimed the event wasn't OD but implied that under the table, it was essentially an Occupy event. Tom was none too pleased about this and others were very concerned about the PR of being connected to this kind of thing. One must remember the PR nightmare that was caused by events such as the Wal-Mart rally, which led to lasting fallout as far as losing participants and supporters.

So it was decided to post on the website a statement that despite rumors in the media, the FTP march was not, in any shape or form, associated with Occupy Denver. Again we argued about punctuation for a half hour but eventually completed the post.

Sunday:

I decided to avoid OD for the day. One has to take a break occasionally right? Even Frodo took a break while Sam bore the ring for a little while. I was watching cartoons, when I made the mistake of reading my email. Marie from Legal was making a desperate shout out for a meeting regarding the arrests the previous day. I was like, "arrests...what arrests?" A quick Google search led to some unwanted information.

Believe it or not, the police didn't want to be fucked. Either that or they didn't like the idea of a mob of masked protesters openly defacing the downtown Well Fargo with spray paint. Or, it might have been the use of urine bombs on the part of these creative activists. In any case, by the end of the day there were five arrests, including some active Occupiers.[15]

I really didn't want to leave the house. I was cursing myself for checking email. But in my role in Finance, it's my responsibility to show up for this kind of thing. I pushed pause on the cartoons and headed for the park. It's funny. I go to the park so rarely now that I get an eerie feeling every time I pass by. Do I feel guilty for having abandoned the occupation? Do I

---

[15] Months later I was told that some of these things were untrue rumors. In fact, Martin, who's an engineer, explained to me that urine bombs (urine filled water balloons) are essential impossible to construct because of the back pressure the balloon would put on your anatomy during the filling process.

miss it? I'm not sure what it is, but I feel the same strange feeling every time I'm on that block.

I drove by while looking for parking but found no one there. I drove by once again and saw no one who looked like they were expecting a meeting. I didn't even see Marie. Oh well, back to cartoons. Apparently I wasn't the only one who had better things to do.

Tuesday:

I went to GA and heard all about the march. The conflict was like nothing we've ever seen before. Most of the protesters were hostile, yet peaceful, expressing their anger through words alone, but there were also rumors of property damage. The police resistance was large-scale and dramatic. They also used more aggressive tactics than usual. Generally the police attempt to respect the right of citizens to march for a while, then intimidate the majority into leaving while arresting one or two examples, but this time it seems they were bent on arresting as many as possible.

At one point they charged the entire group of protesters, attempting to dissipate the group all at once and catch the stragglers in the back. There were numerous stories of small groups or individuals being chased for blocks. Not just followed, but actually chased. Al told a story about how he was isolated and chased down an alley by a motorcycle cop. Just as the police officer began to slow down and reach out to catch him, he grabbed a sign post, spun around and starting running the opposite direction as the police officer flew by. Others told me about narrowly escaping by ripping off their masks and sinking into the crowd of onlookers on the busy street.

I wonder how this incident will be interpreted in the media; did they hear our plea not to connect it to Occupy Denver, or will that association be made? And were the aggressive tactics on the part of the police special for the FTP march, or a turning point in how we are dealt with?

2/29/12

Exciting! I just booked a ticket to Washington, DC for the National Assembly. Yay! I'll be there for two weeks. I also sent an application for facilitating a workshop on "the Mystic Activist."

3/3/12

Before spokes, there was a teach-in on "Occupy Economics." I actually showed up for a meeting, not for the teach-in, but the meeting didn't happen so I hung out for the event. It was taught by this guy Chad who's a professor at a local state university. I don't really know him, but his lectures are good. The most interesting idea I took from it was how he defined class. He makes it structural and essentially discontinuous. There are those who work for money- labor. And there are those who use the capital they already possess to invest, thereby hiring workers and taking a portion of the value added by their efforts.

Last spokes meeting was interesting. It was rather strange because many of the most active participants- Terese, Roshan, Cat, and Liberty, for example, weren't there. As non-hierarchical as we claim to be, I couldn't help but wonder whether a meeting without any of them really counted and I don't think I was alone. The whole meeting had a vibe like it was a less important spokes than usual.

The first topic was how to deal with a recent raid on the Row. The previous night saw a moderately large raid where a whole bunch of blankets and tarps were taken. One young man said he lost his passport. This led to a pretty good discussion about how to deal with these things. Really no one had any ideas about what to do in the short-term so we instead talked broadly about how the GA had abandoned the Row and what could be done about it. It was heated at times and there were no concrete measures taken.

More and more I'm coming to the conclusion that something needs to happen on this front. The GA essentially abandoned the Row several weeks ago. This was the consequence of moving GA indoors, the police moving most of the Occupiers out of the park, and Ben moving on with his life. At the time I thought it was a sad but necessary step. Now I've changed my mind. The Row is still the face of the movement, whether we like it or not. Ignoring it while developing other things is like fixing up a house for sale without replacing the broken windows facing the road.

This all keeps leading me to the same conclusion, which I then deny. It is time for me to start spending some time out there. There needs to be a change and that change needs to start with me because no one else is doing it.

The other big topic at the spokes council regarded bail funds. On Wednesday we held a march downtown which was specifically planed as a non-arrestable protest but between protesters that refused to stick to the sidewalk and police who still remembered the FTP action five days before, things got ugly despite the law-abiding intent. This led to Caryn being arrested. She's one of our serial arrestees. It was her 3rd or 4th time in the hands of the police since the movement began.

This being the case, I brought up the general topic of bailing people out. Can the Legal team do it without asking GA? Are there ever times when we don't bail people out? This was heated but didn't lead to any movement on the issue. There are basically two competing philosophies. Some people say that arrests should be orchestrated, not random and that we should consider being more conservative about posting bail for non-strategic type arrests. The other contingent says that many of these random arrests are caused by the police purposefully creating arrestable situations. It is even said that they target certain people who they recognize from past incidents. From what I hear, this was particularly the case on Wednesday when the police recognized people involved in FTP.

This conversation culminated in an exchange between Paul and Kenny who were sharing a couch on the south end of the room. Paul said something about how we should start leaving people in jail. Then Kenny responded by using a "clarifying question" (which are supposed to be information oriented, like "did you say Saturday or Sunday?") to ask, "So how much time have you personally spent in jail?" The Paul got in his face and went off about how, no, he had never been in jail but had had hard times and his opinion was indeed relevant. That's the short version. Paul took five minutes to say this and did so about six inches from Kenny's face.

3/4/12

The other day I crashed on Tanner's couch. He told some stories from the Wal-Mart action back in December (which feels like four years ago). He was named as having been part of the plan to burn a car in front of the distribution plant.

During this period he and some other Occupiers were headed to his apartment and noticed someone following them. They walked all the way to his house and were still followed. They looked out a window and saw someone with rather poor stealth skills watching them from behind a bush. Tanner opened the door and yelled, "You're not very good at your job, I see you!" The guy came out and claimed to be looking for his keys.

Later, federal agents came to his house and asked him about the Wal-Mart action. They were actually pretty laid-back and explained that 95% of cases like this one are nothing, so they believed his denials.

Last Friday saw the second great Declaration of Purpose session. Like the first, it was long and grueling. Nevertheless, it was positive and everyone seems to feel good about the work we're doing.

For me this process is a concentrated dose of what OD has been all about: ego release and radical cooperation. It's about discovering new ways to work with others and becoming part of a whole. One must surrender one's personal agendas and support the needs and ideas of others, while also honestly representing one's own point of view. It's a constant balance. If you swerve too far to one side you marginalize the points of view of your comrades. But simply becoming passive and failing to represent your views is no better; you owe it to the group to passionately bring your own ideas.

To be honest, this is a challenge with in this book. I don't feel at peace with having this large-scale, solitary project. I keep going because I think, ultimately, it will be a valuable work but working alone like this is the opposite of what Occupy is all about. I've tried to think of ways to involve others but haven't had any terribly attractive ideas. Who knows? Maybe something will manifest later.

I've been planning for some time to include a detailed account of the Declaration of Purpose project as an appendix. I mentioned this Friday to the DOP group and felt kind-of dirty afterward. Who am I to profit off of the work of so many people who are volunteering their energy to OD? I've decided I'd rather make it an independent piece. Perhaps a whole book, written by the whole working group and signed simply by "the Occupy Denver Declaration of Purpose Working Group." I haven't mentioned this to them yet, but they'll probably like it more than me just taking the thing and interjecting it in my personal project as though it were mine.

Due to this project and Occupy in general, my view of group work is changing. For several years I've been pretty down on group projects. It always seems like horizontal structures mask subtle hierarchy; group work slows decision making exponentially; and creativity gives way to bland compromises that no one is satisfied with. I've even gone as far as to become very negative about democracy itself, believing it to empower the lowest common denominator point of view.

I haven't totally changed my mind about these things but I'm starting to see some upside to cooperation. Accountability to others pushes the behavior of individuals much farther than personal willpower. Furthermore, through cooperation you can lean on the expertise of others and specialize in specific areas. This is pretty obvious. The next part may not be.

In deep cooperative work, as we do in the DOP project, the individual ego gives way to a sort of super consciousness or group identity. When you communicate this honestly and sacrifice so much for an interpersonal product, you feel a sensation of ego surrender somewhat similar to that which you may experience in mystical experience. You can feel the presence of a super individual; an individual which contains you and uses you. The group itself is not just a collection of unrelated individuals but an entity which consists of humans. The deeper the communication between the humans, the stronger this transcendent entity becomes. At that point the individuals are like organs or tissues. They still have individuality, but serve the whole. And when one fails to serve the whole, one becomes a cancer to the system.

I first started to perceive this kind of relationship when I learned about how Anonymous works. Anonymous consists of strangers tied only by the internet and a vague philosophic solidarity. They don't have strong personal ties, nor do they have any organizational structures. All of the decision-making is done through impersonal, digital group work; individuals have absolutely no control. It's like the beautiful fractal waves created in chaos theory.

Is this disorderly or transcendent? Some would say that due to the lack of human control, Anonymous is like a disease and is inherently dangerous. I am suggesting that it's more like a super organism emerging from human minds being networked through the digital world just as parts of the brain are networked to transcend the individual parts. The system is out of control from the point of view of the individual human, but not a directionless mob incapable of intelligence. The individuals involved understand that they are contributing toward something bigger than themselves, and retain freedom to move about within the system or choose to leave the system, but have no significant control over the direction of the total organism. The transcendent organism rules itself.

This doesn't mean random swerving around like a car without a driver. It means actual intelligent, linear decision-making with strategy and purpose. And the amazing part is that all of this happens not despite the lack of hierarchy, but because of it. If it was organized with conventional hierarchy, decision-making would be ruled by human individuals and would lose the transcendent quality. I still don't know if this kind of super organism has capabilities individuals do not, but I'm excited to find out.

I'll say one thing right now. The Declaration which is emerging from the working group is far superior to anything I could write myself. It's slow, painful work, discussing and negotiating every word, but it's also invigorating, and at times even inspiring.

3/5/12

Today we held the second church outreach event. It was in southern Denver near my home. It was very positive and we brought in about $200. This group has brought in about $300 in its two sessions this month. That's half of OD's total income during that time. This is frustrating. I feel like I'm the only person in the organization that cares about bringing in money. I asked Terese about asking for donations at teach-ins and she seemed almost offended. I don't know if people think asking for money is counter to the movement, or if they are just lazy about the topic. All I know is that the working group I essentially lead is bringing in half of our income, but all of it goes toward bail. I've been trying to maneuver toward a large-scale flyer printing job for weeks, but every time Outreach comes close to proposing it, someone gets arrested. GGGGRRRRR!!!!

3/8/12

I haven't done a lot of Occupy stuff for a couple days. I'm more concentrated on personal things. I really need to make some money. I made a vow. I will make $500 over and above my church income this month. Here we go! This is not my strongest suit. With this is mind, I'm starting a website that will feature this book and other Occupy stuff.

I feel very iffy about the moral implications of a for-profit activism site, but all I can do is jump in, make some mistakes, and deal with the consequences.

There is a lot of iffy activism out there. I've been reading about financial sponsorship lately. Financial sponsorship is where a non-registered charity receives its donations through a 501(c)3 middle man. The middle-man, the financial sponsor, takes a cut, usually around 10%, in exchange for use of their tax status. Now these guys are doing the charity a favor; their heart is usually in the right place. But they are also profiting on the fact that the charity doesn't have the recourses to register. This relationship is essentially very similar to the relationship between a business startup and a venture capitalist. One organization does all the work while the other one profits simply because it has more capital or legitimacy. Very iffy activism I'd say.

3/13/12

Lately most of my energy has gone toward personal projects. I'm building a website for my Occupy activity called "themysticactivist.com" As most small projects go, this became pretty big once I began. I've been researching self-publishing and selling books online and have begun creating a business model around all of this research.

As I've been doing this, I've also done a lot of soul-searching regarding getting paid for activist work. As I've mentioned before, this is a hard topic. On one hand, if people are going to devote their lives to activist work, they have to be allowed to make a living. On the other hand, paid activism can become a detriment to the very cause the organizers claim to be fighting for.

Here's what I've figured out. Paid activism has an important role as long as it follows certain guidelines:

1) The activity can't be done primarily for the income it produces. The primary goal has to be the cause, while the income is secondary. The attitude must be, "I want to do this activist work. In order to put the kind of time into the work that I want to, I need to make a livelihood from it."

There are a lot of people who have a semi-activist attitude. When asked what they want to do with their lives they'll say they want to help the people, but their primary motivator is still personal economic gain. Saying simply that you want to make your income by helping people isn't good enough, it's meaningless. Truly justifiable paid activism has to come from a stronger stance: I am going to help people and it would be nice to get paid; or better yet, I'll take some money if that's what it takes to devote my life to helping people.

2) The above is an attitude, which is important, but not enough. It must be reflected by the actual economics of the situation. An organization should generally minimize personal gain rather than maximize it as for-profits do. This doesn't mean that activists have to be poor, but they should be taking home less than their for-profit counterparts.

3) The paid activist must be doing activity that isn't going to realistically get done by a volunteer. Volunteers can do a lot but there are certain downsides. They are often less qualified than their paid counterparts. They are also less likely than a paid activist to do time-intensive work for long periods of time. A lot of activism takes many hours of skilled labor and most people who are qualified to do this kind of labor can't be counted on to do it consistently for a long time unless they are being paid. This isn't a matter of selfishness; it's a matter of personal resource. Most people simply are not in a position to give a great deal of time or energy to something that doesn't materially give back.

I think that's about it, but those are pretty big. As long as you follow these, you will truly be giving to your cause in a unique way that can't be easily done for free. This way the money you pull from the cause is a worthy investment rather than a drain.

I'm writing this from Liberty's house. I went to the weekly Outreach meeting, which sucked by the way, and got a call on the way home. Mike On Bike said that someone was arrested. He didn't know the bail yet but it would come anytime, so I turned around and headed here to hangout while we discerned the bail situation. Now it's 1:15 am (three hours latter) and we still don't have word. The information is on the Denver city website. Every few minutes I press refresh hoping the guy's name shows up with reasonable bail. After that, the plan is that I'll head downtown, get the money, and give it to Mike who'll go down to the jail and pay.

There were actually three people arrested tonight and one last night. Last night's was Caryn, who is up to five or so arrests since September. The general belief is that she's been targeted and while I tend to be skeptical about that kind of thing, it really sounds plausible in this case. Last night she was arrested for jay-walking. She was with a bunch of other people, stepped off of the sidewalk for a moment and was arrested 30 minutes later after five cop cars rolled in. They went straight for her and her alone. I heard a rumor that once the police handcuffed her to a city bench and left her there alone for an extended period of time before coming back to arrest her. It should be noted that she is very vocal with police at actions and has gone to many actions, so the local cops know who she is.

Tonight went something like this: there were some people hanging out in the park, Cory among them (the police also know him quite well). No one was really doing anything but several people started filming the cops anyway, just in case things got heated. Pretty soon the cops were ordering people to stop filming, which led to a confrontation with Cory which, one way or another, led to three arrests.

Ever since the Fuck the Police march, the vibe between us and the police has shifted. They are strategically targeting certain people, raiding the Row on a weekly basis, using more aggressive tactics with protesters, and arresting significantly more people. They are often behaving in ways clearly designed to intimidate, and sometimes making what I would call illegal arrests either by purposefully arousing illegal actions on the part of activists, or literally trumping up baseless charges.

Basically all of the police corruption that the cop-haters were complaining about before is now actually happening.

One question that may come to mind is this: why target rabble-rousers rather than organizers? Of the targeted subjects, not one has been a major organizer; they've all been very visible, vocal persons in protests and on the Row but not folks who are in committees. This puzzled me at first but Liberty explained it to me recently. The authorities are more concerned with the Row than with OD the organization. At least for the time being, they don't really care about people having little meetings in bars or at homes, they care about the public displays going on outdoors. While behind the scenes, people like Cory and Caryn aren't particularly influential, they have stature on the Row and are extremely visible during marches. In the eyes of the police, the rabble-rousers *are* the leaders.

Upon hearing this I found myself a little deflated. "You mean the cops don't care about my subversion?" I thought. But that's how it is. Perhaps the organizers take themselves a bit too seriously; or maybe the police don't take us seriously enough. Can it perhaps be a little bit of both?

It could be that these distinctions between organizer and rabble-rouser or between the GA and the Row will get murky anyway. Last night several organizers slept on the street for the first time in weeks. It began in conversation last week and now it's happening. I'm excited about this turn of events. I think it's the right way to go and I'm planning on sleeping (or at least hanging out) down there tonight. We won't use this language for a while but what this really means is that the "re-occupation" is on. It will start small for the first few weeks I assume, but you can mark the night of 3/12/12 as the night re-occupation began in Denver.

Later-

I finally made it home. It's 3:30. We got word about the bail situation at 2:00, I drove back downtown, got the money from the bank, and then went to the park. Caryn was there to receive the cash. She doesn't know me but was filled with gratitude when I handed her the envelope. She thanked me about 10 times. The money wasn't actually for her, but down here in the park, she's a mother figure for all these street kids, and a favor for one of them is a favor for her.

3/14/12

As of today, OD's bank account is official empty. We've suffered several arrests in the last couple weeks and these, in combination with the sleeping bags we bought last week, have completely drained our account. Income has actually been better lately but not nearly enough to compensate for the expenses.

I'm feeling kind-of neutral to this penniless state. For a long time I was tripping about our money situation but now it's like...whatever, we'll just deal with it. This means promotional expenses will either be paid for by individuals or not purchased at all, and the next person who gets arrested will either get help from the DABC or stay in jail. What I'm worried about is May Day. We've been talking about holding a big rally at Civic Center Park with booths and whatnot. This would require expensive permits. Where's that money going to come from?

Last night I stayed in the park. It was my first time hanging out there in over a month and my first attempt to literally sleep there (I've stayed the whole night several times but generally just stay up all night). It didn't go so well- the air was chilly, the ground hard, and the cars noisy. Nevertheless, I was glad to be there.

The atmosphere down there is crazy now. There's far more anger in the air than a few months ago. All over the sidewalk and in the parks on both sides of Broadway there are anti-police slogans scribbled in chalk. "Fuck the Police," "The DPD are terrorists" and my favorite, "Woka, woka. Fuck the copas," are a few examples.

When I arrived at about 1:00 am, there was an ambulance and three patrol cars with lights spinning round. They had arrived because a street person had a seizure nearby. After picking the guy up, the ambulance sped away but the cops stayed. They just sat in their cars watching as a crowd of about 20 young street people got more and more riled up. The kids screamed and screamed at the police. At one point, one of the cops got out of his car and Caryn went up to talk to him. I really thought she'd be arrested for the third time in two weeks but thankfully this didn't transpire. After about ten minutes of this, all three cars drove off.

They then began driving by every five minutes or so. Every time one of them went by, the whole crowd, once again, started jumping out into the road cursing at them. Several times the police slowed down to flip the crowd the bird.

It was surreal. I couldn't believe I was there, and I also couldn't believe that I wasn't more shaken up by it. I mean, this was essentially a little riot. It would not have surprised me if rocks had been thrown or if there had been a mass arrest; that was the energy. And yet, it didn't really faze me; I guess I've already seen enough of this kind of thing that conflict with the authorities isn't as scary as it used to be.

3/20/12

A couple days after the above incident, there was a similar one. In the evening, while we were holding spokes in the park, there were a couple arrests made in connection to a fight. Everyone from the Row, as well as from the spokes meeting, ran down to support those getting handcuffed. Among those yelling at the police was Caryn. After dealing with the three guys, the police turned around, spotted Caryn in the crowd, pushed their way to her and arrested her. To get to her they had to shove several other people aside who were doing exactly the same kind of behavior she was engaged in (yelling at them from a distance). If there was any question as to whether or not she's been specifically targeted, it's been answered now.

That was several days ago and I still don't know what happened to the three. We're out of money so it's out of my hands.

After the incident I pulled aside Benjamin, who's putting the 24/7 Committee[16] back together, and Matt, our main web guy, to talk about putting together a 24/7 page to talk about situations like this one and build sympathy for the Row. Benjamin seemed disgusted by the idea. When he realized what I wanted to talk about, he walked away without a word. Later he came up to me and said that he didn't give a shit about websites and that putting a public face on these issues wouldn't do anything. He said,

---

[16] This was one of the first committees OD organized. It was dedicated specifically to the needs of protesters who sleep at the occupation.

"We simply don't have any solutions, and it's as simple as that." And, once again, he walked away.

This was a few days ago and his words are still with me. "We don't have any solutions." He specifically meant it in regard to the arrests but I've been taking a broader look at this phrase. "We don't have any solutions." We've built these networks and organizational structures and put on lots of events but are we any closer to having an actual strategy for fixing the world's problems?

Some folks, the reformist crowd, will say that you run candidates for office, you write ballot measures, you lobby the government, and eventually real change will happen. But I, like most Occupy activists, don't trust the system. I don't think the existing channels work. I don't think this political system can regulate itself or be saved from within.

Then you also have the radicals who will say more extreme steps need to be taken. But if we had the power to take such steps, we'd already be doing it. The fact is, we don't have the numbers or the money to accomplish full-scale revolution, and even if we did, would it be a good thing?

So what's the third option? If meaningful change can't come from the outside or the inside, how does change occur? What can I say? I'll keep you posted.

One thing I've heard from veteran activists is that you can't win, but you fight anyway. I'm not ready for that; I don't like that answer. I've got a life to live and I don't want to waste it on unreachable goals. If I wanted to devote my life to impossible dreams, I'd go back to playing music.

I've began to see reaching big goals through an analogy of climbing a ladder. So you're looking up at a rooftop, thinking you'd like to be up there. It's 15 feet up; there's no way you can step or jump to your goal. More often than not, we act like flies trapped behind glass, hit our heads against an invisible barrier, never stopping to analyze the situation. There are some goals which are simply impossible or at least impossible, barring the possibility of a miracle. But most rooftops *are* accessible no matter how high they may seem from the ground.

The trick is that once you've established the goal, you need to find a ladder and concentrate on one step at a time. Sometimes you look at the ladder from the ground and you see ten steps. You start to ascend and it turns out that there are actually 20 steps. Often the ladder that originally had ten obvious steps actually has 100 steps. The trick to reaching your goal is to keep the goal in the back of your mind, but put most your concentration on the individual steps. Usually when a goal looks impossible it's because you're paying too much attention to the rooftop and enough to the ladder.

So how are we going to heal the world? One website, one Twitter post, one Outreach meeting, one bailed-out protester, one night in the park, one Facebook status, one GA, one general strike, one debate, one vote, one essay, one documentary, one night at the bar, and one trip to DC at a time. Today I've written about a thousand words. That puts us about one thousand words closer to having a better world. Eventually, as Benjamin purposed, we may run out of steps; the ladder may turn out to be shorter than the roof's edge. But we won't know until we're there, so onward we ascend.

3/24/12

The city decided it needs to do work on the Civic Center Park (might have something to do with all the police cars that were constantly driving over the grass through fall and winter). They fenced the whole thing up; it's all behind a chain link fence now. We had a night or two where no one Occupied the street but with the weather getting better, more and more folks are coming down and staying on the East side of Broadway, where the occupation was when it first began in September.

There's a church I've been in contact with for several weeks regarding putting together an Occupy event. It is a unique situation among the church events we are putting together. My contact person, who is their staff social justice person, was jumping up and down enthusiastic when I first contacted her, but since then she has encountered resistance in the community about working with us. I'd say it's been frustrating for both of us. She has stuck her head out to get Occupy into the church, so she keeps contacting us with questions about who is coming. Ordinarily it wouldn't really matter, but the event she is talking about organizing could have an audience of several hundred people.

She mentioned at one point that the trick to getting something done in her community was to get the support of one particular woman. This seemed a bit strange but I always say we'll do things the way they need them to be done in the individual churches. Well it turns out that this mystery woman is the Governor's chief of staff. My contact recently forwarded this woman our email chain.

This made me start thinking. What's happening to my life? I'm under-employed and have been off and on for most of my adult life. Most of that time, I was some combination of a struggling artist and a student of religion and spirituality. I've been essentially unsuccessful with most of the things I've ever attempted to do; or at least many of them. Now, six months after coming back from China without any real plans or prospects, I'm in negotiations with the Governor's chief of staff. And this is all because of Occupy.

This movement is trying to save the world but it's not obvious whether it can. What is obvious, is that it is saving my life. I feel like I've got all of this passion and talent that is being given the opportunity to manifest for the first time. This is my chance to do something with my life.

3/25/12

Last night there were a couple of dramatic arrests. I wasn't there but I just watched the video on YouTube. Someone put a tent up on the side walk…. one pup tent. And at 3:00 am twenty cops arrived with tear gas and batons out. They organized themselves in two long rows and marched in formation down the sidewalk to remove the tent. They arrested the person in the tent, who was just waking up at the desperate warnings of a friend, and a protester who off-handedly said the tent was his. The whole thing was recorded by Nick at Night who also provided some pretty passionate commentary.

3/26/12

Things aren't so good on the legal front right now. We've got a "Failure to Appear" pending and a pissed off bondsman. We have 72 hours to raise about $300. This isn't a lot of money, but there have been a lot of things lately that don't cost a lot of money and Occupiers don't tend to be rich.

Bonds always go through a particular individual's name, not an organization. This means that if things go sour, one person can be held accountable for the expenses. In our case, more often than not, this person is Cat, our primary legal person. She has put up bond after bond in her own name, sometimes involving her own money, and sometimes the money of OD or DABC. Now, largely due to "Failure to Appears," it's coming back, and in particular it's coming back on Cat. Liberty is desperately putting out mass emails for support. All I can say is that I hope we get it.

I'm getting worried. We've all been talking about "the American Spring" for months. We had to. It was the only thing giving us hope that things would change; that reinforcements were on the way. Now it's spring and reinforcements still haven't arrived. Without the hope of a big beautiful spring and summer, this party will not last.

3/27/12

Long day of Occupy stuff today. First I worked on my website for a couple hours. Then I had my first ever meeting with the "Deconstructing Consciousness" working group, which turned out be just Eli and I, this week. We met in the library and talked for about three hours. We generally went back and forth between Occupy stuff and spirituality, sharing stories and ideas. He was down with putting content from the group onto themsysticactivist.com and linking it to OD's website.

Eli was a monk for seven years in the mountains of Colorado and it is evident in his demeanor and rhetoric. He is almost obsessed with motivating people to take personal responsibility for their actions and problems. I like this, and hanging out with him is a nice break from the more external-oriented crowd which dominates Occupy. I told him that I like him because he makes me uncomfortable; I always feel like he is really paying attention and therefore may call me on my limitations and hypo-crisies at any time.

Something I thought of the other day which is haunting me a bit (lots of "haunting me" lately) is this: what if we, in Occupy, aren't really doing any real activism at all? That is, what if we aren't actually doing anything that can potentially change the world? What if activism is really just an excuse to spend lots of time with each other and that Occupy Denver is really just a social club? I jokingly suggested this to Terese the other day but I'm actually only half-joking. What are we actually doing? How is any of this going to change anything?

Here's Eli's answer: it won't. Eli, like any good mystic, feels that real change starts with the individual and that until people start paying attention to their own minds and taking responsibility for their own lives, mass change is impossible.

My agreement with this is at about 50%. I agree that the mind helps shape one's reality and that people need to pay attention and take responsibility. This is spirituality 101. But there are also external correlates. The internal affects the external and the external affects the internal.

It is true, substantial social change will never happen without psychological change on the part of the individuals within that society, but simultaneously, people are shaped by the culture in which they live. People don't pop out of the womb fully formed with all of their thoughts and preferences already dictated; rather they come out with genetically-shaped tendencies which only take specific manifestation under the guidance of their environment.

The implications that I see for social change is that real change has to occur in both of these realms at once. Change has to be psychological, sociological, economic, and political.

And what pushes it all is technology. It's the advent of the information age which is driving this period of social change. Money works differently than before, communication and transportation work differently than before, and this is reshaping the power balance of our global society. Before the internet there was no WikiLeaks or Anonymous. Before the internet there was no Occupy. The new technology shifts power and as we get used to these new power dynamics, our worldviews also shift. When we realize that due to the new technology, we have the potential to cooperate in radically new ways, we begin to understand that the political limitations of the past no longer apply in the same ways.

As we learned on 9/11, in the new world a small group based on the other side of the world can make an actual, significant military attack on a super power. We learned through WikiLeaks that the secrets of the power center can be exposed and the information can be disseminated. We've been taught by Anonymous that powerful institutions are vulnerable to digital attack. We've learned through Occupy that masses can be mobilized on a global scale.

The evidence is there, but our minds haven't caught up yet. The power center is vulnerable, but we still haven't mentally digested this fact. Perhaps this is the where we begin. It's as Neo in the Matrix said: "I'm going to begin by showing these people a world without rules or barriers."

I think I just figured it out. Everyone knows the world has to change; we just have to prove that it's possible. If people see that real change is possible, they'll jump on board. Ours is a generation of enlightened skeptics. They know the problems. They know these problems are serious. But they look at the past and see failed revolution after failed revolution. They don't commit their hearts to activism because they don't believe it can actually do anything. They don't believe the power center is vulnerable or that the collective worldview can shift. They are wrong on both counts.

In reality, our history is a narrative of shifting and evolving collective worldviews. We change all the time. Even the current culture of skepticism is a relatively new phenomenon, and is in stark contrast to the optimism and patriotism that dominated the mainstream of the 1950's or the idealism of the 60's and 70's.

When shaping a revolution, you have to convince people that a better world is possible, and you convince them of this by showing it to them. Now…what does that mean? What constitutes showing them the new world?

Elements of this revolution:

1) Show ourselves. Before leading a shift in worldview, our worldview must be shifted. We, within Occupy and the activist community, must be shown our own potential and power.

2) Revolution isn't revolution if it isn't moral. People, myself included, must be mentally and morally trained. We need discipline. We need

accountability. And we need loving community.

3) Moral implications aside, this revolution should be primarily non-violent. This is because the new technology evens the playing field in the world of information but not the world of physical might. You shouldn't throw a rock if you can't back if up with an F16.

4) Nevertheless, we are talking about real revolution, not surface level, meaningless shifts. We are talking about shaping our political world to reflect the new power structures. The current top down structure is no longer sustainable; it can't defend itself against the new threats. This means these changes will be radical and long-term.

It should also be noted that changes of one form or another are inevitable. The question really isn't whether we are capable of changing anything; the question is whether we are capable of shaping the inevitable shifts in a direction which actually makes a better world. Revolution is a car without a brake pedal. You, personally, can jump off if you want. You can attempt to steer. You can influence its speed; go fast, go slow. But you can't stop a revolution which is GOING to happen, nor can you manufacture change which simply isn't there.

Later:
    I've been thinking a little more about actual tools for influencing the system and I've thought of something- taxes. What if we started a movement toward a mass failure to pay our taxes? We could collectively make a set of demands and then make the public threat that if those demands are not met, we won't pay our taxes. Has this ever been done before? It's so obvious.
    But there is one problem. Most people have their taxes withdrawn as the year goes so at the end, rather than pay what they owe, they essentially send the IRS a bill for a refund. This means that simply not filing won't do the trick. Could we motivate people to adjust their withholdings to minimize this effect? That would be hard to mobilize and still wouldn't have desired effect. How do people do it when they withhold the portion

which goes to the military? Lots of people do that. Obviously this needs research, but it has potential.

And even later-

Ok, so I just did some research. This method of protest is called "tax resistance" and has a long history. Gandhi did it in the salt tax protest. The only way I could see doing this would be to have everyone fill out a new W-4 and add withholding allowances. This is illegal but is only subject to a $500 fine. This would be much harder than simply having people fail to fill out a tax return but again, in most cases failure to turn in a tax return takes money from your pocket, not the federal government.

If you could mobilize lots of people to fill out fraudulent W-4s, this would serve as a powerful message. Simply talking about tax resistance is one thing but if people were actually doing it with their W-4, it would give the government time to sweat over the reality of the situation. It would send the message that it's more than talk, it's real.

Maybe a more simple method would be to just lie on the W-2 so you get the full refund.

APRIL

3/30/12

I just took a nap after checking in to a hostel in Washington DC. It's a few blocks north-east of the park where National Occupation of Washington, DC (NOW DC) is centered. Today it's about 50 degrees outside- not too bad but a little colder than I was expecting.

The hostel had some confusion over my booking. I swear hostel bookings over the internet always have these problems. Still, it worked out; they found me an extra room and are actually charging me a little bit less than I expected. Oh, except for the deposit. They said at the counter that the internet deposit doesn't count toward the cost of the room…yeah right, since when? I've paid a 10% deposit over the internet for rooms like this about a 20 times and it's always taken out of the total. Whatever, it's a cheap room.

I'm going to go check out the Occupy park and get some food now. Boy, it feels good to be traveling!

Later-

I went down to the Franklin Park, where activities are supposed to be and there were five people there. That was a little worrying, but there was nothing to be done so I didn't dwell on it. I went up and met the five people. This led to heading up north to this big church where the Backbone Campaign was putting on an event. It was led by Seattle based artist/activist Bill Moyer.

This was pretty interesting. There were about five people there at first. The three already talking were glad to see me and my newly befriended companion, show up. Bill was showing a PowerPoint presentation which included quite a hodgepodge of activist-oriented stuff but mostly concentrating on creative methods of protest.

This guy has been involved in some cool stuff! He showed a movie of a flash mob he helped organize where twenty people did a choreographed song and dance number in a Target store. It was like a big musical scene in a Broadway musical. Days before, they had scouted out the store and created schematics of its interior. They created the choreography based on the layout, which included jumping on chairs and counters, and using store items as props; they rewrote the words to a song and had it arranged for a small brass band; they integrated three cameramen into the choreography and organized the shot angles to avoid the inclusion of the cameramen or other techs. They also had several participants wearing lapel mics so the sound of the recording would be of good quality! This was cool! And WAY beyond anything OD has ever done. Look this movie up on YouTube; Bill said it has about 2 million views.

Backbone has mastered the art of creative political expression. They are so knowledgeable about banners, for example, that their training includes instructing people on what tape to use and what stores to go to for materials. They do banner drops over buildings, which are quite common, but they prefer banner lifts, where they attach banners to weather balloons so they can take flight.

My companion was this older fellow named Ken. He had a career in engineering and is a war veteran. Two years ago he had a stroke and now only has partial control of half his body, so he walks slowly and with a noticeable limp. The stroke forced him into premature retirement. He subsequently began devoting himself to activism, an area he'd never shown much interest in before. He explained to me that after the stroke he wasn't sure how much longer he'd live, so he decided to devote what time he had left to leaving a positive mark on the world. His pet issue is fracking[17]. He

---

[17] Fracking (hydraulic fracturing) is a controversial mining technique involving filling the cracks in rocks underground with pressurized water and chemicals to release oil or natural gas.

has stickers on his car and buttons on his vest devoted to the subject. He is also a full-time Occupier in Ohio and is here in DC for the conference, sleeping most nights in his car.

3/31/12

I want to keep up with this journal but I'm so busy! The first NOW DC general assembly happened today at noon. There were about 40 people, I'd say.

It was a bit strange. About half the crowd was in chairs and we set up in a loose semi-circle instead of the usual full circle. We talked a bit about the existing working groups and setting up new ones. I helped set up a group for an inter-Occupy discussion about further steps and coordinated actions and whatnot. About halfway through the meeting, a lot of those on the outskirts started talking amongst themselves. It was weird...just unorganized I guess. Mostly I didn't like the set up with multiple rows that basically constituted an audience. I just had the feeling that a lot of the people there had not been to many GAs.

I met up with Ken and two other Occupiers. After GA we headed up to the second day of Backbone training.

On the way there, I got to know a fellow Colorado Occupier named Ron, whom I first met at the Colorado Occupy event a few weeks ago. He is a huge, frankly scary-looking fellow from Greely Colorado with a tattoo around his neck depicting a circlet of barbed wire. Like Ken, he's a veteran. I believe he was in the second Iraq war and is now stanchly against the American war machine. From his stories, I gather that he is one of the main organizers in the little town.

At the event there were about 20 people working in two groups. One group was studying marching techniques and tactics. They practiced walking in various formations such as stars and windings lines. This stuff is impressive. It's not very complicated but it's organized. These guys are talking about protests that are far more than friendly mobs, which is what I'm used to seeing. In their methodology, every participant has a specific, preordained role.

I was in another group, building props. I began by learning how to build "orca horns." They are these instruments built with PVC pipe, bottles, and balloons that sound a lot like whales when played. Then I went on to help out with big banners which will be hung by balloons in a few days. Others were building huge chain links out of rope covered in black tape. There was also a prop house which seemed to be something like an inflatable castle.

4/1/12

I'm still plugging away with the Backbone folks from Seattle. In addition to the Backbone staff, many of the participants are from Washington, which is kind-of fun since I grew up in Oregon. They are my Pacific Northwest brethren.

Last night was the second of two nights in this hostel. I swear, it must be the worst hostel I've ever stayed in. No Wi-Fi in the rooms. No door knob on the outside door leading to the street. My bed was a crappy little cot which dramatically rose up on all four sides so it felt a bit like a hammock when I lay down. The guy next to me was on a blowup mattress. And the room smelled…fricking terrible.

But hey, at least I had a room and a bed. There was this young Arab American guy staying there at the same time as I. Last night at about 10:00 pm, one of the workers came up and informed him that he had to move. Once again there was a mess up with the internet reservations and they had an extra couple from Italy. Because they had reserved the room two weeks in advance, the staff decided to move this young man off of his bed and out of his room to give it to the Italians. He wound up sleeping on the floor in the hallway outside the door of the room which had previously housed him.

Tonight I'm sleeping in the church where I first met Bill Moyer and the crowd from Seattle. Right now I'm alone in the back balcony of the majestic building. The air is full of frankincense and I can hear the clicks of my typing echo off the tall walls.

Today we met at the library at George Washington University, up on the seventh floor. The first two thirds of the day were devoted to foreclosure activism. The talk was led by some people from Boston who run an organization which buys foreclosed homes at the discounted auction rates in the name of the original owner. That way the original owner essentially gets a second chance at owning the property, only this time the principle is significantly lower. They have done this over a hundred times. They also do lots of canvassing and organize people going through fore-closure into activist associations.

They have this ritual for newbies that's pretty cool. Every so often they hold big meetings with hundreds of people going through the fore-close process. Near the end of the meeting, they bring out a sword and give it to the new person. They ask the homeowner, "Are you ready to fight for your home?" The new participant lifts the sword and says, "Yes, I'm ready to fight for my home!" Then the rest of the people yell, "We will help you fight!"

At the end of the day, Bill gave a demonstration of using a stage light to produce big projections of slogans on exterior walls. This is really cool and I want to do it, but it's not that cheap. The light is easy to rent, they are $25 or $50 for several days of use. For power, you use either a generator or a car battery. But you need an expensive power inverter between the power supply and the light which costs several hundred bucks and are hard to rent. So I don't know when OD could do this, but I know I want to. The effect is great.

The target of the demonstration was a Bank of America. We went out to the institution and added to the bank's messaging. Under the large logo, we projected "SUCKS."

4/3/12

What a couple of days. I'm really tired. We'll…see…how……long ………I…… can……………write……………… .

Yesterday began at 6:30 am on the floor of the church. I slept pretty well, but due to the early wake up, only got five hours of sleep (that might seem pretty good but will become relevant later). Ken, Jesse, Chappel, and I hopped in Ken's car and headed for NW Maryland where a morning foreclosure action was scheduled.

There were about 30 people there, mostly folks who I met the day before at the Backbone training. Bill and his staff were busy setting up their fancy banners. It was pretty funny watching them deal with their weather balloon. It could barely lift the banner and the wind kept pushing it over the road or down to the ground. They also had a huge hand-held banner saying "Foreclosure Free Zone." It must have been 20 feet long and 10 feet tall.

After everyone arrived the 20 or so people who had already rehearsed…so tired…… must sleep…. . . . .

4/4/12

Ok, next day. Despite a three-hour nap, I couldn't write yesterday. I'm pretty good now though.

On with the story: damn, it was cold. DC is colder than I was expecting, or maybe I should say, hoping. The house was in the shade and we were all shivering. We stayed there for about two hours chanting and waving at passing cars. A couple people gave speeches on a portable PA.

The main activity was dancing. Did you expect that? Among the group, about 20 participants had a musical flash mob prepared. It was to the tune of "Splish Spash I'm Taking a Bath," only they changed it to "Splish Splash Homeowner's Taking a Bath." They did it over and over, twirling and singing for homeowners.

I wasn't dancing; I was drinking coffee and trying to stay awake, as was Jesse, who I met yesterday at the foreclosure workshop. She is a college student at Evergreen State in Washington and is writing her Bachelor's thesis on the Occupy movement. Ken, on the other hand, was dancing and singing. There is no stopping that guy! Age…disability…it doesn't matter. If dancing is what it takes to change the world, then that's what he's going to do!

All this happened with cops and moving vans surrounding us in every direction. Around 10:00 am rumors started going around. The owner, who was in court fighting for her house, won the day. The judge ruled that she could keep her house for the time being and the bank was required to continue negotiations. It was a small victory but a victory nonetheless. Bill has a saying he likes to throw around, "Winning is fun." And indeed, this little victory was a great way to start the day.

Next Jesse and I ran off to the Ralph Nader convention we kept hearing about. It was a strange contrast to all the Occupy activity I'm used to. It was held at the Carnegie Institute of Washington, there were stone pillars and caterers waiting out in the lobby to serve us during the lunch break. We quietly snuck in a couple hours late, and found that there were two empty seats way up front, in the second row. We ran down, slipped into the seats, and I quickly took off my sweater and shoved it under the seat in front of me.

After a few minutes of listening to the panel, Jess leaned over said "Do you know who that is in front of you?" Ah, no. Some old guy wearing a suit who has big ears. But then I leaned over to see his profile and sure enough, my sweater was under Ralph Nader's butt! "This is a surreal" I didn't even preregister for this conference, and now I'm sitting directly behind the presidential nominee I voted for 12 years ago.

The conference was cool. It featured lots of well-known activists talking passionately about changing the world. One highlight was the mayor Gayle McLaughlin of Richman, CA. She is highest-ranking politician in the country registered in the Green Party. After talking about all of the work being done in her city, she said something rather provocative. She stated that while she loves the Green Party, she doesn't think it is positioned to make a significant impact on the world and that Occupy should start a party and start running candidates. This would be very controversial in the movement. We are so anti-establishment that there would be a lot of resistance to this, but hey, maybe it's a good idea.

Everything went fine until the fifth panel. This one featured Chris Hedges, the progressive writer, and Kevin Zeese. Before coming here I'd never heard of Kevin, but apparently he was instrumental in starting the Occupy movement, particularly in DC.

After the panelists spoke, they took questions from the audience. Soon some very pointed questions started being asked of Kevin and Chris. One young tattooed man accused Kevin of not being a real Occupier. He explained that he'd never seen Kevin at a GA or down at the occupation and that he thought Kevin was taking advantage of the movement by taking credit for it. Kevin was defensive. He said that if the man had never seen him in the movement than he must not be very involved.

Several other questions were for Chris. Young Occupiers got in line and questioned the attacks that he has made on anarchism and the use of the black bloc tactic. Chris became irate. He went off about his experiences with real war and violence across the world and said that he wasn't so much against violence as violence in this particular movement.

It was amazing. One moment we had an uppity intellectual conference, the next we had an Occupy style, out of control shouting match over diversity of tactics. This went on for about ten minutes with question after question pushing Kevin and Chris, and the two of them getting steadily louder and more angry. Then someone pulled this 80-year-old woman to the stage and introduced her as being a veteran activist and told a story about what happened when she was recently pepper-sprayed. As the story goes, she got pepper-sprayed in her face at an Occupy protest a few months ago. When this happened, she immediately turned to some young men and calmly said, "Now we'll get noticed."

She sat down behind the table on stage, pulled the mic close to her mouth and quietly replied. "I agree that there is nothing wrong with anarchists; but you aren't anarchists, you're hoodlums." Clap, clap, clap, clap, hoot, whistle! The entire audience jumped to its feet and gave her the loudest ovation of the night. After that, the "hoodlums" quieted down.

At the break, some of the anarchist Occupiers got in a big debate with Kevin and some of the other local organizers. I don't know the details of their dispute but I do know it's emotional. It happened around a table with about 15 people pushing up into the circle leaning against the plastic surface. I heard some lady screaming at the anarchists, "What have you ever organized!?" to one man in particular. "I organized the fair we are holding right now!" (The McPherson Occupation is holding a fair to celebrate the six-month anniversary of Occupy Wall Street). This was all I heard. I quickly concluded that the debate was a waste of time and simply headed back into the hall to hear the final panel.

Jesse was already there listening to the first speaker. She leaned over to me and asked what was going on. She said the commotion was audible in the presentation room and everyone seemed to be curious about what was going on. I sighed and explained that it was just typical Occupy shit. She quickly gathered herself and headed out. Since the main focus of her degree is the Occupy movement, she always has an eye for what will add the most important material to her final project. In this case, she made the quick decision that a debate between Kevin Zeese, his supporters, and some Occupy anarchists, was better research material than a stuffy panel about movement growth, even if that panel included Ralph Nader, who was the final speaker.

I'm finding some of my attitudes changing. I'm becoming less tolerant of chaotic, angry behavior than before I left. Ralph Nader, Kevin Zeese, Chris Hodges, and Bill Boyer all make arguments that we should stick to nonviolent tactics. There is a certain element in this movement that wants dramatic, even violent, revolution and they are constantly distracting us. The afore-mentioned people, who've been fighting this war for a long time, have all come to the conclusion that violent, frightening, or chaotic tactics and attitudes are counterproductive. This was displayed at this convention, and I've witnessed it over and over in Denver. These attitudes break up unity, they disrupt meetings, they cost us money, they distract us from our long-term goals, and most costly, they alienate mainstream Americans who ideologically agree with us but are resistant to overtly revolutionary speech and behavior. This isn't about ethics, it's about tactics. Black blocing and other radical tactics and rhetoric are typically counterproductive to actual revolution.

That night I went back to the church to sleep for the night and found Bill and his crew working on the props for Tuesday's action regarding student debt. When I got there they were blowing up the ball, which in 12 hours would represent the totality of American student debt. It was a huge balloon, 11 feet in diameter. Despite its enormity, prepping the balloon actually constituted the easiest aspect of the night's work; just blow it up, throw on a black cover, and you're basically done. It was everything else that was work. Bill, his paid crew, and a group of four volunteers stayed up all night building the other props. This included long chains Ken worked on. These consisted of hundreds of short strands of regular yellow rope looped and wrapped in black tape to look like heavy iron links, and flexible plumbing tubes wrapped in the same black tape to resemble larger links.

Chappel spent all night constructing cardboard graduate hats. Chappel is a middle-aged lady from Tucson, AZ. She is a professional tattoo artist and a full-time Occupier. She's also a little crazy or at least is after an entire night building graduation hats. The next day I hung out with her and helped her navigate life as she dealt with her exhaustion.

My primary job was with banners. We built two banners: one was a simple flag and the other a larger banner designed to be held by two protesters. Even the banners were quite a project. One of my roles was to pick fonts for the text that would be present on the banners. Bill had very specific ideas about what he wanted for the various words and it was my job to go through the several hundred fonts on my computer (Erin and I, strangely enough, are really into fonts and I have downloaded hundreds to my laptop), find a few options, and facilitate a decision-making process. This project alone took about an hour. Then the text was projected on a wall and transferred to the banners. This may sound simple but the process took several hours. By the time the hats, banners, chains, and other props were done, the sun was coming up. This was the second all-nighter in a row for Bill who seemed to be in a delirious trance, 50% caused by lack of sleep and 50% caused by artistic in-the-zone-ness.

The next day, after an hour of sleeping on the floor of the church's gym, I was getting delirious myself. At this point I'd had about 6 hours of sleep in the last 48 hours. That's when I ran into Chappel in a coffee shop. Together we pushed our spent bodies and numb minds to slowly head down to Freedom Plaza where the action was scheduled to begin.

I was recruited to man Bill's smart phone and filmed the livecast. Jesse and Ken donned caps, gowns, and chains. We then proceeded to slowly march down Pennsylvania Avenue with twenty debt-laden students (most of whom were played by retirees), five in-house camera people such as myself, and perhaps another five or so media folks, including people from CNN and NBC. Bill and Jacob (one of Backbone's staff) kept time with mallets on garbage cans while others played "orca horns." The "students" slowly rambled down the street crying, "Help me, Help me" while pulling the great black ball of debt behind them. Around the group on all sides were police officers on motor bikes.

We marched to the Sallie May building and then to the mall were the Capital Building and other official buildings are. While the march itself only had about 30 people, it got plenty of attention. The streets were lined with startled passersby, many of whom hurriedly dug out cameras to record the event. I must say, I have never, ever, ever, ever, been part of anything like this before!

The whole thing was simply awe-inspiring. The Backbone team came with five people and only had a week to work. In that time, they mustered five actions including the foreclosure action, a flash mob I didn't attend, and this masterpiece. It was truly amazing and humbling. It's a testament to what a little know-how, creativity, and funding streams can accomplish.

That night I found a nice hostel about a mile away from the center of activity. It's the same price as the last one but WAY better: clean, great facilities, a good kitchen, big TV, computers, and decent Wi-Fi. Fuck, yeah!

4/7/12

On Wednesday I gave my workshop on spirituality and activism. It was held in the childcare room of a Quaker meeting house. About 15 people were there, all of whom were older than me. Is it silly that I'm not comfortable "teaching" folks you are older than me? Actually, it's only about religious stuff. I don't have this problem when teaching trumpet lessons to older students. The thing is, spirituality is very subjective and personal. It's not about hard facts that are definitely right or wrong. Some people's theological ideas are more developed than others, but it's not a cut and dry topic that you either know or you don't. For this reason, presenting myself as an expert on spirituality to a bunch of smart, experienced folks who are older than me doesn't feel right. In the future, I think I'll try to make it more of an interactive talk and really de-emphasize the lecture portion.

That having been said, the workshop went well. First I guided them in a meditation. This emphasized awareness of yourself, your place in the movement, and your place in the world. Then I gave a lecture about the contradictions and similarities between activism and spirituality. Finally I concluded that, despite some tension, the two complement one another.

After the lecture we took stack. The most interesting part came from a middle-aged veteran who's left arm had been amputated above the elbow. He explained that he has periodic phantom pain in the limb and that meditating was very challenging because it made the pain fire up. He thought about stopping and even walking out, but instead, fought through the pain and had a good experience in the sitting. He felt that the experience of concentrating on his body, experiencing pain, and then facing it rather than avoiding it was an analogy for activism. Activism, like meditation, is about looking at problems and dealing with them, rather than falling into a numb slumber of avoidance. I like this; it was a nice sentiment.

One interesting dynamic at the NOW DC is that the average age is about 60. Occupy in general tends attract young adults in their 20's. This is particularly true among the organizers who fill committees. The second largest group is those of retirement age. We have a lot of baby boomers, whose kids are out of the house, who are working less than full-time, and who are excited to dive back into revolution after a 40-year hiatus. Here in DC, there are very few of the younger crowd, it's all retirees. This is fine of course, but it's an interesting vibe and really separates it from the usual Occupy atmosphere. My workshop was very civil and laid back, lacking the usual conflict and intensity.

Sadly, NOW DC is shaping up to be a bit of a disaster. The Occupy movement in DC is wrought with conflict and factionism. There are literally two separate Occupy DCs; one based in Freedom Plaza and the other in McPherson Park. Worse yet, NOW DC doesn't get along well with either occupation, especially McPherson. This means the majority of local organizers refused to promote the conference. Due to this, there are a lot of holes. No options for housing. No options for food. The Facebook page was down for a couple days in the middle of the conference. And the big caravan that was scheduled to start in Los Angeles and make its way here was canceled.

Get this: the conference got a permit to have tents in Franklin Park and put up several tarps for information booths. Rumor has it, the folks two blocks away in the McPherson occupation, threatened to steal the tarps in the middle of the night, forcing the organizers to pull them down! WTF!? Honestly!

Another problem is the timing. Everyone across the country is busy prepping for the general strike on May Day. A lot of people are also planning on meeting in Chicago in late May so no one wants to travel right now. In other words, no one's here. It's hard to get a count but I don't think there are more than 75 people who came for the conference. We were hoping for hundreds, if not thousands. Sigh…it's very disappointing considering what it took to get here. When these things don't work out it's so depressing. I want…we want success so badly and it feels like it's defeat followed by defeat. I'm really scared about May Day. We've invested so much emotion into that day being a big success and have set a really high bar for what success looks like. If it totally flops, I don't know what will happen.

A couple days ago I heard that there are bus trips to New York for $20.

Fate Hath Led Me to Where it all Started.

I leave tomorrow at noon. Chappel may come with me and hopefully she can score a spot on the floor of her friend's Brooklyn apartment for us to crash on, otherwise it's spending $40 a night for NY hostels.

Despite everything, yesterday was pretty fun. Early in the day we went down to the mall and checked out some of the museums. Afterwards, we headed up to where Ron is crashing, made some food, drank some tequila, and compared Occunotes. It was really nice.

Poor Ron has NO money. He's almost out of cash and he lost his credit card, so he literally has no access to funds until next week when his replacement card arrives. Despite our own economic challenges, Jesse, Chappel, and I have been taking turns feeding him. He's a proud guy and doesn't like the situation, so it becomes a big deal every time one of us buys him something. That is so annoying. It sucks when money becomes an issue in a relationship. Once in China I told a friend straight up, "Look. I make ten times as much money as you do because I'm white and speak English well. It's not fair. It's not your fault. Let me pay for everything and don't trip about it." It didn't really work; she still wanted to pay her fair share for things. It's hard for people to let go of feeling bad about receiving.

Today I spent the day preparing for the trip to New York and then went to McPherson Park for GA in the evening. There I ran into Chappel, Jesse, and Ron. The McPherson Occupation looks great. There are tables and tents dedicated various topics and roles. For example, there is a library with several hundred books and a functional medical tent. The deal here is that the city allows them the tents but they can't sleep in them. They have to leave the park every night and come back in the morning.

Unlike the NOW DC meeting I attended a few days ago, their GA felt like a real GA. Everyone knew each other and the procedures worked like a well-oiled machine. It turned out that this was an important GA as there were two significant agenda items to discuss and vote on.

The first agenda item regarded combining with the Freedom Plaza occupation. The folks at the other encampment want to heal the rift and move their protest up to McPherson. The main controversy in GA regarded not the idea of combining the camps but using a permit for the park. Someone associated with Freedom Plaza wanted to use a permit for the occupation, but this wasn't too popular. It was feared that the permit could be used against them when it ran out. Plus, like many Occupiers, most of the McPherson crowd preferred the "people's permit," the first amendment of the Bill of Rights.

The second agenda item involved Kevin Zeese and his partner Margret Flowers, who's a well-known healthcare activist. The tensions between the McPherson occupy and these two have come to a head. I talked to someone from the McPherson Finance Committee recently about the situation who claimed the two stole several thousand dollars from the occupation. Someone later told me that the money they pulled from McPherson was actually money they'd themselves donated.[18] I don't know the facts, but I do know it's a mess and that the emotions are very hot.

After the confrontation at the Nader conference, Kevin and Margret asked for permission to come down to the McPherson Occupy to discuss their problems. The proposal the GA was to vote on was not whether or not to issue this invitation, but whether or not to discuss issuing such an invitation. The question was whether or not issuing permission to show up was worthy of a proposal or not. Theoretically it was purely a matter of procedure but, boy, was this bureaucratic discussion charged!

The stack went 25 or more deep. Everyone had an opinion and the conversation kept veering from the actual procedural question to talking

---

[18] I went on to work with Kevin and Margret after the conclusion of this journal and get to know them fairly well. Kevin explained that there were constant rumors spreading about the two of them during this period. He feels that these rumors were most likely started by infiltrators from the Democratic Party and allied non-profits like Moveon.org who wanted to bring Occupy into the partisan, Democratic fold.

about issues with the individuals involved. Margret and Kevin had never been officially voted off the island, so there was nothing keeping them from showing up. They didn't need permission, so why should the GA give it to them, some argued. The thinly veiled subtext was, "Who the fuck do they think they are? Why should we give them special treatment? If they want to talk, they should show up to GA like anyone else."

I went on stack, waited my turn and attempted to give an outside perspective. I said something like this:

"Anyone can come to GA and speak; you don't need permission. This is central to Occupy and therefore a proposal to give permission to show up is redundant. But the GA exists to organically deal with the issues faced by the occupation as they come up. I don't know the details of the situation but this is obviously a really big deal to you guys. It's my opinion that while the proposal is strange, it is the GA's function to deal with strange situations. Be realistic, these aren't some unknown strangers quietly show-ing up to GA. If these folks show up it's going to be a really big deal, so it is important for the GA to address it beforehand."

Despite the controversy, the proposal came to vote after an hour or so of debate. The vote didn't get to far though. The facilitator first asked if anyone wanted to block[19] the proposal, and to everyone's surprise, some-one lifted his arms and crossed them in an X across his chest signaling a block. He then explained that a proposal to give special permission to attend GA is against the fundamental values of the Occupy movement, and hence, block worthy. This was the only block I have ever witnessed in an Occupy general assembly.[20]

---

[19] Most occupations have a "block" as one of the voting options. It is sort of a super no. I've heard two definitions. The first is that you use a block if the proposal is so offensive that it threatens your continued involvement in the movement. The second definition is that it is used when the proposal contradicts the essential values of the movement. How a block is treated varies, but generally it automatically stops the vote, at least temporarily.

[20] I never heard what happened with the proposed meeting with Kevin and Margret. The combining of the two encampments did go forward, but only temporarily. It was not long after I left that the park was cleaned out by the city police, ending the physical occupation of Washington DC.

4/8/12

I just got to my hostel in New York. I'm excited to be here. I've always really liked this city and I think it's a great turn of events that I would end up here.

This hostel though. Man, I've had some bad luck with hostels on this trip. They messed up my reservation so I had to prove I belonged by pulling up my reservation email. Then I looked around for a kitchen and found none, not even a microwave! So now I'm trying to make ramen with cold water from the bathroom sink. Oh yeah. Why not use hot tap water? There's no hot water. Dude. How can you provide no microwave AND no hot water?

Anyway, I'm glad to be here, although eating may prove to be challenging. Now I just have to figure out why I'm here.

4/9/12

Last night I went down to Zuccotti Park[21] for GA. To my dismay, there was none. Nevertheless it was a pretty heavy experience being there. The park is tiny. It covers a very small block and is surrounded on four sides by enormous skyscrapers. There is very little grass; it is covered by concrete and a few flower beds. Despite the absence of a GA, I was hardly alone. It was full of police and tourists taking pictures in the now famous little plaza. I'd estimate that there were about 15 cops hanging round on routine scouting duty.

I was upset that there were no Occupiers there. "Is this what has happened to our movement?" But two things should be noted. First, most Occupying in New York is now done in Union Square, a mile north. Secondly, it was Easter Sunday. I took a few pictures, sat and soaked in the moment, and walked off.

I soon ran into The World Trade Center Ground Zero. It is about a block to the west of Zuccotti Park. There is a big area fenced up and off limits. There is also a large plaque depicting firemen with the names of people who died on 9/11 covering the bottom portion of the bronze plate. It reads "Dedicated To Those Who Fell and To Those Who Carry On. May We Never Forget." Like in Zuccotti, there were numerous police officers

---

[21] This small park is where the original Occupy Wall Street encampment was located.

and foreign tourists. To the south, the adjoining buildings appear fine and many have lively bars on the street level. To the north and north east is construction for several blocks; these areas I assumed where damaged during the attack 10 years ago.

I walked a couple blocks south east and ran into the New York Stock Exchange and Wall Street. That area has several small one or two lane streets which are blocked and guarded. Like the other two areas, there were bored cops every few yards. Walking through here I felt nervous, like I was on a covert operation and it was imperative to hide my identity. I walked past the huge Chase building and noticed a little sticker within the "e" in "Chase" on the street level sign. It was a cartoon about greedy bankers.

From southeast to northwest, you've got the New York Stock Exchange, Zuccotti Park, and Ground Zero, all within a diagonal three block line. To the southeast lies the problem. To the west can be found the symptom, in the middle is an honest attempt at finding a solution.

Back in DC, on my last night, I got in a conversation with the general manager of the hostel where I was staying. He asked what I was doing in Washington and I told him about the conference. He then started going off...oh man, I've heard this before.

He told me about how "you guys" shut down traffic on Pennsylvania Ave for several hours, stopping traffic and being a huge nuisance. "I supported you guys until you did that." He explained.

"You really fucked up!"

"I wasn't there sir, I'm from Colorado."

"Yeah, I know that, but you're an Occupier. You guys really fucked up. And before that I was sympathetic but no one is going to support you now. You can't inconvenience people like that. People were stuck on their cars for five hours."

"Yeah, well. We are growing and learning. Sometimes we make mistakes."

"No, you are done. When you did that, you were done."

This morning I ran into an article in the Huffington Post about how the Democratic Party successfully co-opted the Occupy movement without giving them any seats or integrating their message. The article compared the triumph of the Democrats over Occupy to the Republicans' inability to ignore the Tea Party. Part of this argument hinged on Occupy Wall Street being a thing of the past and repeatedly talked about it in the past tense. What am I trying to say here?

Over and over, people don't seem to comprehend what's at stake. The attitude of the hostel general manager is all too common. "You should have done this. You should have done that. If you had, I'd support you. If you had, you'd earn my esteem and perhaps even my contribution, but you've proven yourself unworthy of my time, energy, or respect."

Ok, sorry. I want to apologize in advance. You know how people will get in your face, pretending that you are someone else because they aren't courageous enough to actually confront the person they have a problem with. That's what I'm about to do to you; my sincerest apologies.

Look. In early 1940's, the US made all kinds of mistakes. It probably inconvenienced the drivers of Washington DC all the time. It probably did a lot of stuff that was a lot worse. But people stayed with it. They stayed with the effort because they realized that confronting the war machines of Germany and Japan was an imperative. They sent their young men off to die in the war. They put innocent Japanese Americans in concentration camps. They aligned themselves with Joseph Stalin and created the world's most terrifying weapon. A weapon so horrible that we fear it's potential to destroy us all to this day.

But despite these facts, the vast majority of the population stuck with the war effort. They not only supported it, but contributed in any manner they could, despite significant sacrifices.

These times are no different. We are fighting to save our country. We are fighting to save our planet. But people don't get it. They get pissed off because we slowed down traffic for five hours. I'm sorry your kid didn't make it to soccer practice, I was too busy saving the planet from economic and ecological catastrophe, and forgot to personally call you up and warn you about the protest.

And the media. It's the same shit. Now I'm not a big "blame the media for everything" guy, but I am getting frustrated. It feels as though the story about how unsuccessful the Occupy Wall Street movement WAS (past tense), was written about an hour and half after the original protest began. These journalists come up with a convenient story, run with it, and pretend their actions don't have consequences.

This dude says we were co-opted by the left. WTF is he talking about? Occupy hates Democrats almost as much as they hate Republicans. When a Democratic politician uses Occupy language, they either get ignored or find protesters outside their office the next day. This being the case, how have we been co-opted? And as far as us not influencing the political climate...dude, there hasn't even been an election yet.

All of this shit comes down to one thing: people make excuses for not being involved. They say we made critical errors. They claim the movement has already died. They suggest that it is violent, radical and dangerous. Some of that stuff may be true but under the hood all those claims come from scared souls justifying staying on the sidelines. They pretend this isn't a big deal. They pretend getting involved isn't worth their time. They suggest that Occupy is a run of the mill, special interest group or young people's fad, but in reality this is a war for a better future, and the stakes are just as high as during WW2 or any other crisis we've ever faced.

Perhaps we've made mistakes. Perhaps I've personally made mistakes. But I'm fairly sure that if this all fails, it'll have a lot more to do with that journalist publishing the movement's obituary as early as possible, and that hostel general manager deeming "you guys" unworthy of his time than the mistakes of committed activists...Ok, I'm done ranting.

4/10/12

Today I went downtown to Union Square, on 14th street. This is the new location of Occupy Wall Street. I was feeling rather cranky and shy. And feeling cranky and shy only makes me more cranky and shy.

It took me a couple minutes to find the occupation but eventually I walked into a huge Occuparty. There were perhaps 250 people chilling there, mostly in small groups. There wasn't any special event going on or anything like that. This is simply how it always is.

There was a food table where dinner was being provided. When I was in line for the cornbread and rice dish some lady with a NY accent was bitching that no one was donating so I put in a couple bucks before claiming my food.

There were several information tables. One was general Occupy Wall Street stuff, presumably associated with the GA. This table was covered with flyers, mostly dealing with May Day. I took a copy of the Occupy Wall Street Declaration to compare it to Denver's and check out how they published it.

There was also a table for a local anarchist group. They were also giving away several flyers and pamphlets and advertising an anarchist book sale. There were a couple of jazz musicians, one on tenor sax, the other on trumpet, playing free music together. The sax player was much better than the trumpeter, played on a better horn, and left before the other musician. My impression was that they didn't actually know each other before meeting that day at the occupation.

There were also a couple of groups of young black men dancing. They kicked ass and one guy in particular really blew me away. I concentrated on his feet as he moved and tried to imagine my feet moving like his. Eventually, I sat on some steps and began meditating. I wasn't alone in this approach to occupying; near me were several young white men doing the same.

After a half hour or so I heard some Indian raga-style chanting begin. It included a harmonium, some hand drums, and several people chanting "Hare Krishna, Hare Krishna." Soon the sax and trumpet joined in the music to make a jazz-Indian hybrid jam session. It is times like this that I really miss my instrument; playing with these guys would have been a truly fun event. Their sound rose and fell for about an hour. Occasionally the musicians stopped and onlookers clapped.

Later, about half that group broke off, made a circle a few feet away, and meditated together, sitting Indian style with their hands on their knees.

It was about this time that a troop of about a hundred protesters carrying Trayvon Martin[22] signs entered the park. They gathered at one sign and started passing round a mic attached to a bullhorn. It kept feeding back and sending screams across the plaza.

And that was my experience at the famous occupation of New York City. It's basically a big, multi-generational, multi-racial, political hoopla. It's a permanent party. Really, it was pretty impressive considering that it was a totally normal day.

---

[22] Trayvon Martin was an unarmed, 17 year old African American male, killed on February 26, 2012 in Sanford, Florida.

4/13/12

Day three in New York was a complete waste of time. I went to MOMA, the famous art museum and had a good time (although I didn't come here to go to art museums). As in my past trips, my favorite stuff was on the fifth floor, which is where the really famous work from the dawn of modern art is held. They've got several Picassos and van Goghs, including *Les Demoiselles d'Avignon* and *Starry Night.* One thing that struck me on this trip is how those guys had contemporaries who worked closely with them and were as much part of the art scene as they were.

The icons we make, Martin Luther King, Picasso, Charlie Parker, get too much credit. We write history as though it's a story of a few great individuals but it's not really like that. Each of these icons was part of a movement, they didn't work alone; but our minds don't see things that way. Our brains are designed to keep a few dozen individuals in our world. They've done studies that found that people struggle to keep the relationships of more than about hundred people in mind. This makes sense. In a hunter/gather society you wouldn't know more than a few dozen people.

To simplify our complicated histories, we boil down movements of thousands of people to key individuals. It's easier mentally, but creates an illusion. It's an illusion where Charlie Parker, Pueblo Picasso, and MLK shape the world while the rest of us passively watch. We idolize them and wonder what makes them so great, but in reality it's as much our own way of viewing the world that makes them great as any special qualities they had.

After the museum, I went down to an indoor public area on Wall Street were OWS holds a lot of internal meetings. I was hoping to find a group there dedicated to long-term planning and creating goals, but they were nowhere to be found. I did find their Education Committee though, which had about 15 people, all of whom were teachers. They spent most the time planning for May Day.

They had an interesting discussion about student walk-outs. Someone mentioned telling students about the strike and attempting to motivate the students to walk-out. The problems, they all agreed are these: If the administration get wind that a teacher is promoting a walk-out, there could be serious professional ramifications. In fact, several of the teachers complained that they didn't feel permission to talk about Occupy at all in the classroom and admitted that they tend to hide their involvement.

The other problem is that while convincing students to skip school is easy enough, the vast majority simply see it as an excuse to go home, while only a few care about politics and participate in protests. One of the teachers talked about a conversation she'd had with a student organizer who lamented that her classmates didn't seem to care about the issues and were difficult to mobilize.

I didn't speak at the meeting. Frankly, by this time I was so down on the trip that I began going into my introvert shell that I sometimes escape to. Once there, I can go months without meeting anyone and I feel powerless to shift the energy. So I left the meeting completely depressed about my trip to the east coast, Occupy, and life in general. One thing happened though. I made a decision. I decided that this trip to New York wasn't about networking or promoting my websites, it was about taking a stand myself.

One thing I've never done is do a solo political action. I'm not really a solo kind of guy generally. I don't like public attention much and I don't really like looking funny in front of people or making people uncomfortable. Furthermore, even in the context of being with a lot of like-minded souls, I tend to put less emphasis on protesting than other Occupy activists. But I respect those who can say, "I'm going to make a statement, even if it's just me making it." I like that kind of courage and openness, and if there's one place to make a public statement, isn't it New York City?

So I devised a plan. At first I planned on doing a protest outside St. Patrick's Cathedral. I would have a sign like, "Demand that the church take a stand on corporate greed" or something like that and sit in front of the church while praying the rosary. I haven't actually prayed a rosary since I was like 19, so I looked it up and man, that thing is complicated. A bunch of Hail Mary's I can do, but there's a lot more than that. I thought about desperately trying to memorize it all, but I knew I didn't have time. The plan would have to change.

In my four trips to New York, for some reason, I've never gone to Liberty Island to see the Statue of Liberty up close. I think I always figured that it was better from a distance so I skipped the short trip. Now on this trip it seemed like a perfect opportunity. I planned to take the ferry out to Liberty Island, plant myself on the grass somewhere with a protest sign, and hope I don't get arrested.

4/15/12

Yesterday I got up fairly early and headed down to the south end of Manhattan where the ferries leave. But before I left, I needed a sign. I Googled for office supply shops and found several in the area, but when I walked into the first one, I found the store to be tiny and not to have poster-making materials. Then the second, same thing. The third, same thing! Finally I walked about 10 blocks north (totally out of my way) to find the nearest real supply store. I was so frustrated at this point! I wanted to be on the island as long as possible but now it was pushing noon and I still didn't have tickets. The store had a really long line and I just stood there steaming in my frustration about the situation. Fucking New York with their fucking canceled committee meetings and GAs, and their fucking lack of office supply stores downtown, and their fucking overrated pizza and overpriced, crappy hostels and $10 minimums to use a credit card!

I got to lady Liberty's island home two hours later.

Now my shyness started to kick in. What am I doing here? How have I become the annoying weirdo sitting alone holding a sign? At first I looked for every excuse not to hold my protest. I walked all the way around the Island; I took some pictures; I sat and meditated for a while. But I knew what I had to do and that prolonging the wait simply prolonged the stress. I went to a bathroom stall to make my sign.

I'd actually been struggling to think of the perfect protest signage for about 3 weeks. It had to be serious but clever; simple but meaningful; pointed but non-confrontational; and it should include a suggestion, not just a complaint. While sitting in the bathroom stall, I scribbled across the poster board, "Help Us Help Everyone. Occupy May 1st."

I found my spot in the grass on the east side of the island facing Manhattan, with lady Liberty to my back. I sat down with my back leaning on a big tree and held my sign with both hands. I was so uncomfortable. I couldn't look up; but I quickly found a solution. I pulled up chess on my phone and played the game, doing my best to forget where I was. A lot of people looked at me as they walked by; a couple took pictures. One group offered me money but I didn't take it.

But this scene didn't last long. After one or two distracted, losing games of chess, my concentration was broken.

"We need to talk to you for a moment sir."

I looked up to find two police officers peering down at me.

"We don't mind that you're here, but I'm pretty sure you can't have a sign like that" Said cop one.

"So you want me to leave?" I said, trying to sound friendly and compliant.

"No, no. You can be here. But we're pretty sure you can't have a sign" he answered.

"Hey, I don't want to cause trouble, but I need to know whether I HAVE to put away my sign before doing so. Is it illegal or not?" I said, frustrated.

"I think you should just put away your sign, sir" interjected cop two.

"OK." I said, "Here's what we'll do. I'll stay here with my sign and you go find out what the ordinances are to see if I'm breaking the law. Then come back and tell me to move after you are sure you've got the authority to do so."

Cop one. "Umm"

Cop two. "What do mean, 'if we have the authority?'" as he twisted his head to the side a little.

At this point I came to the conclusion that I'd pushed them hard enough. I don't have any contacts this side of the Mississippi and don't have a legal line to call. I folded up my sign and slipped it into by backpack. We talked about Occupy for a few minutes. They asked if I thought we were actually helping the world. I said that at least we were trying. Cop two mentioned that he didn't have a problem with political protest as long as it didn't get in the way of business being done.

They left after about five minutes, and five minutes after that, I did as well.

4/16/12

This was the end of my New York trip. The next day I took a bus back to DC. There was a mix up with the bus. They said my reservation was for the wrong day. This was stressful. Everyone else sat down in the bus, while I stood there desperately trying to check my email on my phone but the 3G was way too slow and the buttons too small for my nervous fingers. By the time everyone else was seated, I was still trying to navigate the internet to find proof that I belonged with them. A dozen people watched as I had a temper tantrum, cursing my phone for failing to bring up the page I desperately wanted. Finally some lady jumped off the bus and informed me that the reservation could be changed for 1 dollar. I can change it for one dollar! Why didn't they just tell me that in the first place? Oh well.

This scene took place right next to a movie crew filming a big crowd of extras pretending to be excited about someone showing up at the nearby hotel. As I stepped onto the bus, a limo drove up and out popped Howard Stern, waving and high-fiving people to the brilliantly performed exuberance of the large crowd. Sorry if this story came out of nowhere, but it really happened. This is how I left New York City, the Occupy Mecca of the world.

That night I slept in the chapel of the Ronald Reagan International Airport. I had a bed in a hostel but could only stay there for a couple hours due to my flight leaving too early to use the metro in the morning. Since there was no way I could afford a taxi, I had to stay in the airport all night.

I spent all of my money. My checking account had $10 in it by the time I made it home and my credit card is now about $500 further from freedom. There was essentially no conference, instead just in-fighting among local occupations. I hardly met anyone. I hardly marketed my projects. I learned some, but not that much. And to be honest, I feel worse about the movement now than ever before.

I'm not sure specifically what it was about this trip, but the problems and criticisms are beginning to affect me. All we do is march and complain. There are no real plans, goals, or strategies, just anger. That's not to say that there aren't themes to our grievances, there certainly are. But these have not solidified into actionable strategies. We still haven't gone beyond complaining. Furthermore, three fourths of our energy is spent tripping out about purely short-term, tactical concerns such as raising bail funds. All too often, the forest of social and economic issues gets lost among an endless number of "Fuck The Police" trees. And while many Occupiers don't seem to notice, everyone else does, and consequently our popularity in the general population continues to dwindle.

I'm not in a big hurry to jump back in. I'm looking at my email and just not wanting to read it. After reading it anyway, I don't want to reply. Someone asked me about some earmarked money that went missing and I was like, "I don't know. Whatever. It's gone, too bad for you." I want to continue with activism but there has to be a better way.

MAY DAY

4/22/12

I've been back in Denver a week now and am back in the thick of things with the occupation. There are three topics dominating everyone's work.

One is a proposed city ordinance banning urban camping. If passed, it will be the end of the physical occupation and will give the police justification for arresting any homeless people sleeping outside within the city limits. OD is pushing hard to fight this law; I get email everyday on this topic. We have teams writing letters. We've had meetings with city council people. They've had two or more meetings a week dedicated to this topic. We've even had meetings with the official who wrote the proposed ordinance. I've stayed completely out of this work so far.

The ban totally sucks for the homeless of Denver but I'm not convinced it would be bad for OD. If we were forced to totally abandon the physical occupation, we could move on to other tactics and move on with our lives.

The physical protest is now at an all-time low (it always seems to be at an all-time low). It's bigger than in the winter but the atmosphere is different. It's a party every night now. Ever since it moved back to the east side of Broadway, it's been inundated with drugs. Hard drugs. On any given night there'll be people drunk, stoned, tripping, on meth, or heroin. And when the police are called for an emergency, the call is sometimes ignored for several hours. The thought is that the police don't like the occupation (big surprise there) and simply don't want to serve those people. The scene is totally out of control.

Last week I was at GA when a recent addition to the Row, named Revolution, added an agenda item to the docket. We went through all the procedures and had him introduce his proposal. He proceeded to give a ten minute speech about how the GA should allocate funds to his friends and him so they could go buy booze and drugs and party all night. He was serious! Everyone laughed, someone handed him a smoke, and then we went on to the next agenda item while he complained that he wasn't being taken seriously.

The second thing we've been working on is May Day. I'll tell you. I'm really worried that we're going to have like 60 people participate. OD feels more and more like a club and less like a movement every day. Everyone is pushing hard on this project. This is our first coordinated, cross-committee campaign. It's the first time that literally all of the organizers are pushing the same project and this, I believe, is a great development. We are heading toward the kind of coordination we need to make habitual. I really hope that after May Day we move on as a group, to another project that we all dive headlong into. Ultimately reaching this stage in our evolution is more important than the general strike itself.

This confirms a theory I have. I believe that people are amazing, wonderful creatures that perform amazing acts of creativity and adaptation. But we are also lazy and short-sighted. We only adapt when we are forced by outside circumstances to do so. When there is a threat, we quickly evolve to the point of being able to meet that threat, but we don't do it without substantial negative or positive reinforcement. People don't like to change but they will when they have to.

For example, let's take the threat of nuclear war. The bomb came about in the 1940's when there was a race to invent and produce the technology during WW2. As soon as we built the incredible weapon, we used it. Records show that there was no debate about the ethical implications of the weapon's use. The allied military leaders didn't have a single conversation where they considered whether or not they should bomb Japan; everyone involved simply took it for granted.

After the war, the technology quickly spread to several other countries and two nuclear powers in particular began stockpiling thousands. At that point something amazing happened, something that in thousands of years of human conflict had never happened before: despite our intense continued conflict, we didn't use our most powerful weapons. We held ourselves back. We developed a level of global intelligence and discipline we'd never before had. Due to the threat of mutual destruction, we developed international organizational systems such as the United Nations, and the internal self-control to avoid global catastrophe, and began, for the first time, to develop the concept of global identity.

This, I believe, is how nature pushes us forward. We are presented with challenges, many of which are actually caused by our own actions, and we discover systems, technologies, and philosophies that help us deal with those challenges.

For Occupy Denver, May Day represents a new challenge. For the first time ever, we are in a situation where everyone involved is required to pull off a large project that is universally seen as a really big deal. It is demanding that we cooperate in new and better ways, both internally and with other groups as well. We are in partnership with the IWW, the International Workers of the World. We are printing at both P&L, the print shop associated with the DABC, and SQWGLZ, which is run by Deacon from Outreach. We have multiple poster and flyer designs. We have buttons. We have organizations and committees putting together booths. We have businesses showing support. We have multiple dedicated webpages. We are attacking this like we've never attacked anything before. This is why I am deathly afraid of the consequences of failure. I think a terrible event could kill this movement.

The main role I've given myself in this effort is flyering. Once I dreamed about coordinating a large flyering effort with a dozen or so people, but everyone is busy. I've simply taken flyering on a mass level as a personal call. I've given myself the goal of personally distributing 1000 flyers for May Day. Last week I started printing some at home. I bought some semi-fancy paper and cranked out 120 in two days. Then my beloved printer broke. I started inquiring about more flyers but haven't found an adequate supply. At this point I'll estimate that I've flyered about 250 houses. It's not enough. I really want to reach that 1000 mark, but there just aren't enough flyers about. I might print a few myself at a copy shop.

The third big topic people are working on is our legal situation. Occupy Denver owes a bondswoman $1200, payable at the end of the month. If we don't pay, all of the bonds that we've done through her will be pulled and there will be a warrant for the arrest of everyone out on bail. That could be dozens of people.

Consequently, the legal committee has been desperately raising funds. On April 20, legal spent all day on this effort. At the park, OD sold baked goods all day. In particular we were out in force at the 4:20 pm celebration which attracted hundreds of hungry stoners.

Then we had a big 4/20 bash in the evening at an art gallery. After a couple hours of flyering I arrived at 6:00 pm. There weren't too many people there but there was fun in the air. When some confused-looking musicians came in lugging their gear, it became evident that while we had a simple PA, we didn't have a soundman. It just so happens that one of the two dozen or so jobs that I've held in the past was as a soundman in a church, so I volunteered to take that job. This was fun. I haven't ran sound in several years and it felt good having some responsibility. The job itself was easy, but I kept forgetting that I was supposed to be doing it and people would occasionally find me and say, "Dude, we are switching bands, get up there." This happened three times! Damn it, I blame Al! Every time I hang out with that guy I lose brain cells.

The good news is that Jesus loves you. The other good news is that legal brought in about 1000 bucks on the day so reaching the goal should now be easy. One less thing to worry about.

4/23/12

It's late, I'm tired. Time for bed, but first some writing. I went to outreach tonight. May Day was the only topic. Nothing that happened made me feel any better about the event. No outside groups are joining us at the fair portion of the event. We were hoping for lots of outside groups to jump in and have tables or booths but it hasn't happened. This is a bad sign. Even the Thunderdome is out so we have to find another way to provide food. I'm at 250 or maybe 300 flyers that I've put up. I only have eight days to put up my final 700.

We are also talked about doing some banner drops. Nice banners cost money so banner drops can be risky because your expensive banner may be confiscated by police or damaged by weather or traffic. But I've got an idea. Instead of fancy professionally constructed signs we'll use paint on cheap paper. We'll hang them up somewhere nice and visible and instead of picking them up after a while, we'll just leave them, like you would a conventional flyer.

I also agreed to email churches. I just spent four hours sending a form letter to churches while watching Buffy the Vampire Slayer. It's all first season stuff, which I haven't seen in several years so it's pretty fun. I emailed about 75 churches. It sounds like quite a few but I don't think it's enough.

I don't quite know what it was about today's meeting, but something happened that triggered my cynicism. I now believe that May Day is going to be a disaster. We're going to have 100 people, just like NOW DC. I can't explain why I feel like this but that's how I feel. We didn't organize it soon enough. We didn't get enough help from other organizations. And most importantly, we don't have enough support in the community. Most people have given up on us and don't care if we organize a big event. For most people Occupy is over.

4/24/12

Today I went to GA. It was my first time to the park in a week or so. The encampment has really grown. It's the largest it's been since last November; there must have been close to a hundred people on the street or sitting in circles throughout the park. It was nice to see, but in reality it is fairly separate from the GA and it is questionable how connected to OD all the activity is.

There has been some talk of me helping this fellow from Occupy Faith, the national Occupy religious organization, to do a workshop at the

May Day Fest we are putting together to accompany the strike. I asked Terese about it today and she said the May Day working group is still deciding whether it is appropriate for the event. Some, included Terese and Roshan, are positive on it but others have reservations. Some argued that a teach-in about religion isn't on topic because the themes of the event are labor and cooperation between organizations. From what I was told, there were also a few people going as far as to say that religion and Occupy are incompatible. There's another meeting tomorrow and Terese said she expected the teach-in to be approved, but this touches on something that's bugging me more and more.

In the beginning of this movement, we represented the 99%. We were mainstream, or at least tried to be. The one group we were very tentative about including was institutionalized liberalism, that is, the Democratic Party. Over and over we made stands against the Democratic Party and avoided the co-option that brought down the Tea Party. But in doing so, we became unfriendly to the mainstream liberals who were filling our ranks.

Now we are putting together this big event that is supposed to be for the people, but in reality it is super leftist. There is no money allowed; it's "a day without money." We told the Green Party they couldn't participate because they are partisan. And now the case of this teach-in…no religion allowed? Why is the *people's* movement constantly pushing people out? I'm afraid that while we set up all of our defenses against co-option from the Democrats, anarchist leftists came in through the backdoor and pushed everyone else out.

4/25/12

I'm not going to make my goal of distributing 1000 flyers for May Day. One reason for this is a lack of flyers. PnL printing has promised to supply as many simply black and white flyers as we can use but early on there was a shortage. We'll see; maybe I'll go out there and pick up some more but I'm not sure I'll get around to it. At this point I'd estimate that I've distributed 300 or 400. I'll bet I get up to 500 by the end.

I spent another night emailing churches. Here's the process:

Step one) Start an episode of Buffy the Vampire slayer on NetFlix.

Step two) Google Map "churches in Denver."

Step three) Move one at a time through the little orange dots searching for links to church websites.

Step four) Open the site and look for an email address to use. These are usually in a "staff" or "contact" area.

Step five) Copy the address into the proper area, delete all the extra stuff, and forward the official May Day email.

This process takes an average of about three minutes, so a lot of Buffy gets watched.

I think everyone in the occupation is suffering right now. The weight of May Day, in combination with the urban camping ban is too much to deal with at the same time. Terese is front and center in both these efforts. Yesterday as she stared past me into space, she told me about how she keeps catching herself doing silly stuff like forgetting her keys or putting sugar in her juice instead of her tea.

4/28/12

May Day is in two days and OD is bustling with last-minute preparation and marketing although personally, I've pretty much given this project what I have to give. I emailed a couple dozen more churches, flyered a few hundred more homes, a put up about 20 of Deacon's fancy posters.

I also did the banner work I was talking about a few days ago. Chris G, and Don, who are both on Outreach, joined me to make 13 tall skinny, paper banners which read "May Day," and "Strike," and a few other simple messages. We then drove down to a nearby busy street and lined both sides of the one-way road with the banners. As the cars flew by, we placed a chair next to each telephone pole, climbed up to get some extra height, and taped the colorful, painted paper strips vertically on the poles. We did this on all the poles for two blocks. The effect was dramatic. For two blocks drivers were bombarded with simple little statements on both sides of the road.

We chose to paint them all in different colors and to make them unapologetically simple, even child-like. The idea was that the simple quality would lend a since of fun to the effect.

I find myself really proud of this project. During the first day alone, the banners must have been viewed by thousands of drivers, and by lining them up one after another after another the effect is far more dramatic than with a single poster. Plus, the materials were very cheap, just a few bucks. The packing tape for attaching the banners to the poles was the most expensive element. The project makes me appreciate the training I received in DC with the Backbone Campaign. Their philosophy of creative, dramatic use of simple statements has obviously influenced me and I feel far more confident and capable of creating effective messaging than before.

After the last GA, what remains of the severely over-worked Terese pulled Roshan and I aside and announced that she needed to vent. The topic was the Faith teach-in. Despite her support for the workshop, the May Day working group decided not to include it in the May Day festivities.

As she described it, they circled around the real topic, suggesting that it simply didn't seem relevant but the thinly veiled opinion of the group was that religion itself is counter to social change. Many of them were proud atheists and simply didn't support organized religion.

Afterward it was up to poor Terese to email the would-be facilitator and tell him that he wouldn't be able to give the class. She did so as politely as possible, saying there wasn't time on the schedule, and invited him to do hold the class at a later date through the Education Committee. I was CCed on it and read the message. It was well-written but seemed fishy. I wasn't surprised to learn the truth in Terese's less edited version that she gave Roshan and I.

She complained about the attitude pervading the group, and lamented that she had been essentially alone with a dissenting opinion. Roshan mentioned that the evils of fundamentalist ideals are not isolated to Christians or Muslims and that even atheists can give in to such arrogance.

… Indeed.

Christopher Mandel

I was not surprised by any of this but nevertheless angered. Angered beyond words even. Dumbfounded. I asked Erin later that night if she'd ever found herself so angry that she wasn't angry. Instead of being moved to swing fists or profanities, you are simply quiet and numb. Perhaps vaguely sad, but not blowing fire from your ears. These are my friends, colleagues, and brothers and sisters in the great struggle, but what can I say? Their leftist intellectual elitism is going to destroy this movement, if it hasn't already. It's really no more complicated than that.

4/29/12

I went down to the park today and hung out with Nick at Night and a few of the other people down there. It was sunny and there were lots of people around; it was fun. Everyone seems excited about May Day and there was lots of positive energy. Later I went to a last-minute meeting for the big protest. This was fun too! I guess I was just in a good mood today, and it was nice see a few folks I haven't seen in a while.

There was a couple there from "Occupy the Road." This is a hippy motor home that travels around the country visiting occupations. The right side is covered with Occupy posters and the left is devoted to Bradley Manning.[23] They are here for May Day and are planning on following around the protesters during the march. They suggested that someone could hang out on top the vehicle while they slowly drove down the road, like in Teen Wolf! Awesome, let it happen! Let it happen!

I figured out my role in the march. Ever since we started this movement, I've wanted to run around in a mask playing my alto clarinet but I've never done it. I think the time has come. I practiced a little today to get ready; it was ridiculous. It's been so long since I've played that my lips ached with exhaustion after about 45 seconds. I changed to a softer reed which made playing much easier, so hopefully I'll be ok. I also could hardly remember my basic scales. Ok, before you say I must totally suck, keep in mind that this isn't my main instrument…I remember my scales on trumpet, so just shut up! As a solution to this problem, I focused on C blues and G major. These should be good enough to rock out for a while.

---

[23] Manning is the army private accused of providing WikiLeaks with secret documents. He's currently in military custody.

I'm also planning on playing electric. I've got a batteries powered guitar amp and a hiking backpack I bought in China. These, in addition to a mic and an echo pedal will mean I can play live, solo electronic style. The pedal even has a built-in drum machine so I can have a rhythm part in addition to stacked up, overlapping clarinet parts. This is going to be totally fun! What should I wear?

4/30/12

April 30th was a really nice day. First off, I got paid. Remember I was totally broke after the DC trip and was living off of Erin and a credit card ever since. Let me tell you, after two weeks of this it felt amazing to switch back to my debit card.

The main project of the day was to build my suit. I already had all the essential parts but figuring out the subtleties of putting a guitar amp on my back and an effects pedal on my belt wasn't easy. At first I thought I'd put the amp in my backpack but, alas, it didn't fit! This was a major turning point in my plans. I considered completely building an alternative strap system but instead I simply smooshed the bag down and strapped the amp on with adjustable belts. Next was the little effects box. While recording audio loops, one's performance with the device's buttons has to be precise. If you push the main start and stop button too early or late, it will ruin the music. But remember that the main button is built for feet, not hands, so it has a very heavy lever. My first several tries at strapping it to my torso didn't yield satisfactory results because the main button was too difficult to push down with exact timing. It wasn't until the third attachment strategy that I found a system that worked.

Another issue was reeds. The alto clarinet is a fairly rare instrument, so reeds are generally not carried in average music stores. I once ordered a box over the internet from a major music dealer, waited several weeks for their delivery, only to receive an apologetic email that stated that they couldn't obtain what I wanted. For this reason, I've been using a bunch of worn out reeds, that I didn't even like when they were new, for about three years. This has actually limited the amount I use the instrument.

Therefore, I really didn't expect to find any replacements in town but thought I'd call around just to make sure. Yay! I received great news on my very first call. They not only had reeds for the instrument, they carried two brands and about four strength levels. I raced down to the store, bought several 2 ½'s and 3's, and came home to try them out. All but one were far better that the old sticks I've been playing on and the instrument immediately became easier to play. Now with these new reeds and a functional amplification backpack, I was ready to rock this May Day event.

May Day

I arrived at the park at about 12:30 pm on May 1st, already in musical mayhem garb, including the backpack, the large clarinet strapped to my chest, and a gold mask with tinsel hanging from the edges. I was also wearing a black belt with a plastic sparkly buckle which read "love" in plastic jewels (I bought this belt for a dollar in a cheap jewelry store for teenage girls in Beijing about a year ago). In the little pavilion near our regular meeting place, there were several tables, a stage, and about 300 people.

When I got there, some organizers were explaining the proceedings to the crowd on the PA. Soon after this, we broke into a huge GA and took stack to allow people to speak. This was perhaps the largest GA I've ever seen and the group had to huddle in close to hear everyone. The most notable speaker was Matt. I haven't seen him since he and Kylie showed up a few weeks ago looking for a place to stay for the night.

On this day he was wearing his familiar red bandana over his face and spoke not for Occupy, but for Anonymous. He announced that the online network is calling for a series of actions across the nation, at various corporate head quarters across the county. He took several minutes naming off the specific locations and dates being called for. This is all in response to the House of Representatives passing CISPA, the Cyber Intelligence Sharing and Protection Act, which is the latest attempt to legalize online surveillance. It was nice to see that Anonymous had a presence at our strike and great to see Matt and Kylie standing in the circle.

After the informal GA, it was announced that we'd begin the march. I was excited but had a problem; I couldn't reach the "ON" switch on my amp. I pulled aside Mike on Bike and asked him for help. He turned it on but I didn't have any sound. NOOO! This always happens when you're dealing with music gear. I made an adjustment. Still no sound. WHY!? One more adjustment. YES, SOUND! Time to go.

Due to my technical problems, I started out way in the back of the march and struggled to catch up because of the weight on my shoulders. Nevertheless I was immediately having fun. One thing I really love about playing music is that it brings out another personality in me; often a personality I prefer. When I'm playing, particularly if its improvised music, I shed my shyness and insecurity. I'll squeak and squawk, I'll rip my shirt off, I'll jump off-stage and run around the audience. I love who I become when I'm making up music.

This was no different. I played with everything I've got, including the stuff I know annoys some people, without tripping about what people thought.

After 15 minutes I managed to get to the middle of the crowd. There was a drum troop of about five marching percussionists leading the chants and lending a beat for the crowd to enjoy. I based most of my playing on the beat these drummers laid down and often matched the various chants with my clarinet.

We were mid-way through the march, circling past Broadway and Colfax when suddenly I heard commotion behind me. I couldn't see what was going on but there were several cop cars with lights going and about a third of our protesters were crowding around the area while the rest pushed forward, stopping traffic while crossing Colfax. The back section was turning around to confront the police. One of our internal marshals starting shouting for them to ignore the police and keep up with the rest of the protest. I turned away from them so that the speaker on my back faced toward the group and began matching the marshal's instructions with my microphone, which up till this point had been sitting in the up turned bell of my instrument.

I have no idea if my pleas influenced anyone's behavior, but the offshoot soon turned back around to join the rest of the crowd. Behind them they left one young man in handcuffs and a small group of lingering protesters screaming at each other.

We then headed north to the 16th Street pedestrian mall. Having spoken through the mic once, I now felt more comfortable with the idea.

Plus, my lips were beginning to get tired from blowing on the clarinet, so I started leading chants as we passed through the busy tourist district. At one point I let someone else use the microphone. A young guy beside me was screaming a chant at the top of his lungs so I walked beside him and held the mic up to his mouth so he could get more volume. Soon we stopped at the Federal Reserve Building. There, several people took turns giving speeches and Tanner led us in some "bring down the evil empire" stuff. It was all very radical; far more radical than was originally planned for the day. As a matter of fact, we weren't even supposed to be here. What the hell happened to the march plan?

Why did the OD marshals change the plan at the last minute? Oh I see. They didn't. Way up in front of the march I saw what was going on. Another group had jumped out in front of the OD banners with their own banners and was directing the path of the crowd. You've got to be kidding me. Guess we'll just have to deal with it.

We then started back toward the park. I continued playing my instrument, occasionally stopping to join a chant or simply allow myself to take a break from blowing. By this time exhaustion was starting to set in but I felt moved to push as myself as hard as I could. As the march went on, my playing became progressively more extreme. I was matching chants with deep growls and gliding over the top with high pitched screams. Guys like Tanner get as radical as they want on their bullhorns so I can do likewise with air passing over a reed. Or so the logic went in my head.

Near the end of the march we found ourselves walking down the middle of a street the police had failed to clear of vehicles. I was bewildered but really had no choice but to weave between the stopped cars. Imagine this from the point of view of the drivers! You are stopped at a red light when all of a sudden your car is surrounded on all sides by protesters. 20 foot banners go by; a drum corps goes by; scary punks in Guy Fawkes masks go by; people screaming on bullhorns or making funny faces at you through your rolled up window go by; a 15-foot Statue of Liberty puppet goes by; finally some weirdo with a gold mask, an over-sized clarinet, and a Ghost Busters backpack goes by. I'm sure a lot of those drivers were thankful to also see the long line of bicycle cops pedaling along beside the protest!

After an hour of marching, we were happy to make it back to the park without any more major incidents and I was glad to pull my backpack off and drink some coffee.

The rest of the day went well. We had two sessions of multiple workshops which were fairly well-attended and enjoyed. We had several bands and speakers, including Siddique Abdullah Hasan, the famous prison reform activist on death row, speaking via telephone.

At about 5:00 pm I had to pack up and leave because there was an important event at my church: several of my younger students were receiving the Sacrament of Reconciliation for their first time. During the ceremony the children went up to the back of the church, one at a time, to confess their sins.

Afterward the adults were invited to do likewise. I haven't celebrated this sacrament since *my* first time when I was 10 years old, and have secretly regretted this ever since. So I walked up to the back of the church and confessed that I was guilty of many sins. The priest wanted something specific.

"What have you done that has made you believe that you were isolated from God's love? In reality," He explained "God's love is never withdrawn, but sometimes we do things that make us feel like it is. What has made you feel this way?"

I replied that I am often guilty of sloth. I am often too lazy to fully express who I am capable of being, and in doing so, I prevent the world from seeing one of God's many beautiful lights. The priest explained that even Jesus was tempted to sin, and that it is by living life, not by bypassing it, that Jesus became great. And likewise, it is by passing through life's challenges, and even our own mistakes, that we can become fully human and holy. He then gestured the sign of the cross and pronounced my sins absolved.

I headed home, drank a beer with Erin, and then drove back downtown for the second half of the day's adventures. A last-minute addition to the May Day plans was a "Sleep-In" on the 16th Street mall. This was meant as an action in our ongoing resistance to the upcoming urban camping bill. I parked near the art museum, where I generally stash my vehicle, and walked the half mile up to the 16th Street mall with a backpack full of random overnight gear, a tarp, and a sleeping bag.

I was a bit concerned at first that I wouldn't find anyone, but fear not, the protest was not difficult to spot. I walked down the pedestrian mall for a couple blocks and saw a crowd with sleeping bags on the sidewalk and center walkway. There weren't tons of people but those who were there were certainly visible. As I got closer, I realized that I knew over half the people present.

In urban camping, the tarp is important. You put it under your sleeping bag to protect it, and if you fear precipitation, you wrap it around you to protect you from the sky as well. Cardboard is important too if it's cold. It'll protect you from the chilly ground and can be used as a wind barrier. However this night was perfect. It was dry and warm and there were good spirits among the group of friends.

I laid my stuff down and started talking and having a nice time. It's great when political actions are fun and, thankfully, this is actually the case most of the time. Everything was great. There were no cops around. Strange, actually. But there were several security guards who worked for the nearby businesses watching over us.

By 1:00 AM the scene was beginning to quiet down as folks started laying down in their sleeping bags and dozing off, when out of nowhere, a man ran into our midst and threw a brick he'd been holding through the glass door of the "Sunglasses Hut" right behind our encampment!

Then he ran off into the darkness in an attempt to incriminate Occupy for the crime!

No, he didn't.

Then he jumped into the store and filled his pockets with sunglasses!

Nope, not that either.

He just stood there grinning at us. He was a young, shirtless white guy, probably 20 or so. He had black paint covering most of his exposed skin, like a vaudeville dark-faced singer from the 1800's. Everyone was immediately freaking out. This was an attempt to ruin our action! This incident would be construed by the media as part of the action and added to the long list of crazy things the public associates with Occupy Denver!

Within seconds, a dozen people jumped up with their phones and started filming him. He started posing and dancing around for the cameras, still with the crazy smile on his face.

For 15 minutes this fellow stood there clowning around when finally a police car came around. This is downtown Denver, mind you. There is absolutely no way that the nearest police unit was 15 minutes away, but whatever.

When they finally did arrive, they took one look at him, and informed us that they deal with this guy all the time. They took him off in their car and left us with a half dozen security guards, the owner of the sunglasses store who wasn't too happy to see us there, despite our innocence, and a bunch glass covering some of our sleeping bags.

The rest of the night went fine. We talked and laughed. I ate a 7/11 burrito. And I eventually headed for my spot on the sidewalk. And finally, after six months in the Occupy movement, I managed to fall asleep on the sidewalk. I heard the next morning that at 5:00 AM the local media showed up, interviewed a few people, and covered the scene live on the morning news.

EPILOGUE

7/11/12

On May 14, the Denver City Council passed the urban camping ban with a 9 to 4 vote. I was at the proceedings. The crowd was so big, they had to open a large overflow room where people watched the action on large TVs. There were lots of boos and cheers from the passionate crowd of homeless and homeless advocates. It felt a bit like watching a hockey game at a sports bar.

At one point, one council member sarcastically asked the crowd to stick to reacting with up and down twinkle fingers instead of all the noise. It was a sad reunion. Ben and Dana were there (they'll be having one of the nation's first Occubabies soon). Mary from my church was there; we shared our first-ever hug after the meeting.

This was the final blow to the physical occupation between the State Capitol and City Building on Colfax. Nick at Night, Mike on Bike, and a number of other homeless activists headed to the mountains to take a break from urban life. Liberty and her boyfriend Silas are also headed to the mountains soon, so the Occushelter is gone. The park still has people in it every day, but it's not an occupation. I haven't seen a protest sign out there in weeks.

Nevertheless, the organization is still plugging along. We've put together several decent marches since May and our tactics continue to improve. On most weeks, we hold three teach-ins; we still have two GAs a week (although attendance isn't near what it was a few months ago); and all told, there are probably ten or so OD committee meetings a week.

Since May, we've broadened what we can put together. We organized a large multi-day camping trip; we hosted an Occupy caravan coming through town; and we've tabled at several festivals.

Perhaps the most proud I've ever been of Occupy Denver was our participation in the Denver PrideFest, which is one of the largest Pride festivals in the country. We marched in the parade with a float dedicated to the marriage of Lady Liberty and Lady Justice. We built big puppets of the two icons, and put them on the back of Martin's pickup truck holding hands. We then decorated the truck with streamers and tied lines of empty cans to the back like the two were running off on their honeymoon. We had several big banners and a big poster of Lady Liberty and Lady Justice making out. We began the march with Chris G formally performing their wedding. We had four people wearing big puppet heads that looked like Supreme Court justices which the local "Move to Amend" chapter brought. The judges moved about through the crowd giving away stickers and flyers.

The rest of us chanted Pride specific slogans which, like usual, were led by people on bullhorns. I once again donned my clarinet/gold mask outfit. The event was perfect. Great, clever messaging; lots of event-specific stuff to give away; quite a few people; relatively militant, but no conflicts; and no arrests.

I just got back from a trip to Philadelphia where the movement's second attempt at a national gathering was held. It was great. Kevin and Margret from DC were there and Chris Hedges made an appearance as well. There were several hundred Occupiers from around the country in attendance, most of whom slept in the parking lot of a Quaker house. On the last day we marched with about a thousand people. The tactics were fantastic. There was music accompanying most of the chants, there were hand signals for quickly communicating stop, go left, slow down, etc., and they worked smoothly. When things got tense with the large police presence, everyone remained calm and communicated well. It was a march of a thousand strangers but there wasn't a moment of mob mentality. These people may not have known each other, technically speaking, but they were all veterans of dozens of protests and had a group identity as Occupiers.

A journal is not a novel. There isn't an obvious place to end implied by the narrative. There is no, "The End." But nevertheless, one has to end it at some point or else the book won't have a back cover.

May Day constituted a major turning point for Occupy, at least in Denver. The coordination which went into the event marked a shift for the movement. Back in the fall, we were a heap of fish on the deck of a ship; each of us thrashing about wildly but unable to actually move, cooperate, or get anything done. In the seven months between October and May, Occupy Denver became an organization, a functional entity capable of planning, strategizing, and execution. In the fall, we didn't know each other, we had no proven techniques, no infrastructure, no experience, and no binding group identity. By the time May Day rolled up, all that had changed. We were still young and far from perfect, but we had the structure, knowhow, and culture to put together a great event.

May Day also marked the end of our significance in popular culture. Despite the efforts of dozens of people, only 300 bodies actually showed up for the march and festival. 300 people do not constitute a "general strike."

A lot of people talk about everything the Occupy movement did wrong. People talk about specific mistakes Occupy Denver has made. But that's not actually the problem; not in my opinion. The problem is that in today's world of ten-second sound bites, and 15 word Tweets, public awareness and political mobilization is done in short bursts.

The days of slowly building momentum as you create relationships and the word of your activity spreads is over. Information doesn't travel by horseback or even public mail; it travels at the speed of electrons passing through strands of wire.

We are in a new age of activism, in which popular movements happen in bursts, which have a predictable life-cycle of a few weeks. We have seen this over and over in the last couple years.

The Wisconsin protests. In reaction to governor Scott Walker's Wisconsin Budget Repair Bill, which among other things, was an attack on public unions, hundreds of thousands of concerned Wisconsiners and their allies marched in the streets and occupied the State Capitol building. The first day of protest was on February 14th, 2011 when a group of University of

Wisconsin staff sent the governor protest "Valentine's Cards." Two days later, there were over 30,000 protesters on the Capitol lawn. By February 18, it was 70,000. The protest plateaued at about 100,000 people and had its largest crowds on March 12, when as many as 185,000 people were present at the capitol.

The movement was fairly stable until June when it suffered a series of defeats, including Walker's bill being upheld by the state supreme court. At that point the protest quickly died down to a few hundred activists.

Kony 2012. On March 5, 2012, a short film named *Kony 2012* was released on YouTube by the small nonprofit, Invisible Children, Inc.. The film was a professionally produced, propaganda style documentary about the exploits in central Africa by warlord Joseph Kony, and laid out a plan for how American youth could convince the government to arrest the villain.

In the two weeks following the release, the movie was viewed 75 million times, and by March 30th it had eclipsed 100 million views. Stinging criticism of the movie and its creators came quickly. The movie was attacked for lacking balance and scholarly accuracy, and Invisible Children was accused of various forms of corruption. On March 16th one of the founders, Jason Russell, was detained for public masturbation and this news spread across the country just as fast as the movie had, just two weeks before.

The film called for a large day of action on April 20th. This was a mixed success; there were small gatherings around the country and thousands of posters put up. Around that time I saw several around Denver. I also ran into a couple anti-Invisible Children posters.

WikiLeaks. Led by founder and spokesman Julian Assange and pres- umptive whistleblower Bradley Manning, the website WikiLeaks.org released the largest trove of secret American documents ever exposed to the general public. Beginning in April of 2010 and climaxing in November, the group released literally millions of military and diplomatic documents and film files. When their entire collection of diplomatic files was released, it became daily national news for weeks as various media sources around the world sorted through and reported on the contents.

While many of the documents contained embarrassing or even illegal activity on the part of diplomats and politicians, the main story in the news was WikiLeaks itself. Assange was soon implicated in a sexual misconduct case in Sweden and put under house arrest in Britain. Manning was arrested on May 26th, 2010 for, among several charges, "aiding the enemy" and has remained in military custody ever since.

Beginning in October 2010 and continuing to this day, the banking industry has maintained a "financial blockade" on WikiLeaks. The industry as a whole, including PayPal, Bank of American, Visa, and MasterCard, refuse to do business with the organization and since the implementation of this tactic, WikiLeaks has found it impossible to remain financially stable despite having millions of supports.

In response, Anonymous conducted a series of cyber attacks on companies associated with the blockade, and there have been hundreds of related protests.

Trayvon Martin. On February 26th, 2012 George Zimmerman, a Hispanic man in his late 20s, shot and killed the 17 year old black teen, Trayvon Martin. Police arrived soon after and Zimmerman immediately admitted to the killing. He was taken into custody but then released the same day.

Two weeks later, a stranger, who read about the killing in a newspaper, created a petition on Change.org, calling for Zimmerman's arrest. The petition garnered over 10,000 signatures in the first few days and eventually got over 2.2 million. On March 13 through 15, the story hit the national press; stories appeared in the Huffington Post, and the New York Times, among several other major news sources.

The first rallies for Trayvon were around March 20th. Soon there were protests taking place across the country and media figures including Barak Obama, Carmelo Anthony, and Al Sharpton jumped at the chance to show solidarity with Martin's family. The protests soon died down after Zimmerman's arrest on April 11th.

These recent events are very diverse but show certain similarities which form a pattern. Modern movements have a particular life-cycle. How this cycle manifests varies greatly depending on the circumstances, but there is enough commonality to postulate a predictable form:

Here are the basic stages I see happening in these events:

1) The fire starter. Someone does something. Contrary to popular belief, it doesn't have to be big; it doesn't have to involve thousands of people. In fact it generally doesn't involve more than a handful of folks doing something which is somehow fascinating. It may be unjust and despicable, like the killing of Trayvon Martin or courageous like WikiLeaks. It may be clever, like a tent city on Wall Street. It may pull your heart strings, like the Kony movie, or it may be that your political enemies have gone too far this time, like in Wisconsin. In any case, there is some kind of unique event which serves as a catalyst.

2) Mass media attention. The tool of the activist is independent media, but this tool must be used to harness mass media. Modern movements don't catch fire until Fox and CNN are paying attention. The case of *Kony 2012* is interesting. The movie came out on YouTube; lots of people watched it; because so many people watched it, it was covered by the mass media; due to the media coverage, more people watched it.

3) Public excitement. After the media informs the public of what is going on, a stage of public excitement occurs. A certain segment of the population is so excited that they are moved to get involved. This leads to more media coverage, which leads to more excitement. The story spirals into a movement in which thousands of people are getting involved and millions are paying attention. This spiral could be called a wildfire, but in some cases that would be an understatement. This stage can be more like an explosion.

4) Disillusionment. The system is dependent on the mass media, and the mass media is not in it for the long haul, nor are they dedicated to the success of the movement. They are quite willing to abandon the story

as soon as public interest begins to wane, and they are also willing to manufacture side stories to keep interest going, including negative storylines. In the cases of *Kony 2012* and WikiLeaks, this came in the form of sex scandals. For Occupy, it was exaggerated depictions of violence and premature proclamations of the movement's defeat. During this stage, the movement, which only days before was a symbol of courage and a source of hope, becomes controversial and ambivalence replaces exuberance for most of the general public.

5) Decline. After a few weeks, depending on the circumstances, media attention wanes. Those who were likely to get involved have already done so, and jumping on board at this point is no longer the cool thing to do. Even if the movement sustains its numbers, as was the case for several months in Wisconsin, the story has already dried up for the media and most of the public. The excitement is gone, and attrition will invariably outpace recruitment.

All of these movements began with an iconic event which captured the attention of the media and imagination of the public. Over the next several days to a few weeks, involvement and attention grew at a dramatic, exponential rate. Finally, often following some bad press, the movements began to die down.

Kony had the quickest, craziest path; 75 million views in the first two weeks, and largely dead after two months, but they got what they wanted. By March 20th, 15 days after the movie was released, Congress was talking about Joseph Kony on the floor of the US Capitol and working on a resolution for amping up attempts to find the man and dismantle his forces.

And that gets to the point I'm trying to make: *Kony 2012* was successful despite the inevitable decline phase. The final phase is simply part of the process. Occupy didn't do anything wrong, it was a hugely successful tactic.

So how do you measure the success of the Occupy movement? The most popular answer is that it "changed the national discussion." You hear this all the time. Occupy Wall Street interjected the topics of economic inequality and corporate money in politics into the national dialog. Now those things are on the radar of most Americans.

This answer is fine, but I think there's a better answer. There is a form of success that is far more important that no one is talking about because they haven't noticed yet. The true success of Occupy Wall Street; the profit which the Occupy investment has yielded; the reward for all of the sacrifices of the last nine months…is me.

A year ago I wasn't involved, now I am. The success of Occupy is Terese, Tom, Nick at Night, Liberty, Roshan, Mike on Bike, Cat, John, Al, Caryn, Crazy Jesus Lady and all the other Denver Occupiers. It's Jesse, Ron, Ken, and Chappel. It's the Thunderdome. It's our relationships with the DABC, the IWW, the CPC, AIM, and Move To Amend. It's occupydenver.org, occupytogether.org, interoccupy.net, and all the other websites we've built. It's The Occupied Wall Street Journal, the Portland Occupier, and the other journals that have appeared.

No one really knows why, but there was something about the original Occupy call to action that inspired thousands of people, not only to show up with their tents, but to change their lives. And while hundreds of thousands of them eventually went back to normal life, a few thousand did not. They are still going; still fighting. And even the people who did head back home when it got cold were changed. They met a few people and learned a few skills. Through Occupy, there is an entire new generation of activists dedicated to changing the world; dedicated to nonpartisan resistance to the status quo.

While the news teams have left for the time being, our relationships have not, nor has the infrastructure we built. Our media contacts, email lists, bank accounts, and legal lines are still up and running. Unlike last fall, there are thousands of people in this country, most of whom are under 30, who know how to write a press release, how to start a petition, how to construct an event page on Facebook, how to build a 10-foot tall puppet, how to pay a bond, how to start a co-op, how to build a banner, how to design a quick flyer, how to serve food for free, how to schedule a meeting with the Mayor, how to think up a chant, how to raise an emergency $1000, how to sleep on the street without getting your sleeping bag dirty, how to build a quick, easy website, how to shoot video while walking, how to put music to a chant, how to livecast from a phone, and most importantly, how to organize a bunch of strangers while minimizing rigid hierarchical structures. The next time a hundred thousand people decide to show up, we'll be ready.

One last thing, on the way back from Philly, Terese and I finished the Declaration Of Purpose. We haven't taken it to GA yet so it's not official but I'll let you see it early:

Occupy Denver is dedicated to fighting
economic injustice, political corruption, and corporate greed.

ABOUT THE AUTHOR

Christopher Mandel lives in Denver, Colorado with his wife, Erin. He received a Master's of Theology from the Iliff School of Theology in 2010. Since 2011, he has dedicated most of his energy to the Occupy movement and other forms of activism.

ABOUT THE PUBLISHER

Occubooks.org is dedicated to creating revenue streams to non-traditional charities, while providing an alternative to conventional online bookstores. Occubooks.org has a large, general catalog of hundreds of thousands of titles, as well as a small number of in-house publications. A significant proportion of all sales go toward charity.

www.ingramcontent.com/pod-product-compliance
Lightning Source LLC
Chambersburg PA
CBHW030017290326
41934CB00005B/371